THE MODERN NATIONS IN
HISTORICAL PERSPECTIVE

ROBIN W. WINKS, *General Editor*

The volumes in this series deal with individual nations or groups of closely related nations throughout the world, summarizing the chief historical trends and influences that have contributed to each nation's present-day character, problems, and behavior. Recent data are incorporated with established historical background to achieve a fresh synthesis and original interpretation.

The author of this volume, RUSSEL WARD, is Associate Professor of History at the University of New England, New South Wales. He is the author of *The Australian Legend,* which in 1961 was co-winner of the Ernest Scott Prize for the most distinguished work in Australian, New Zealand, and British Colonial Pacific history published in 1958-1959. He contributed the keynote chapter to *The Pattern of Australian Culture,* edited by A. L. McLeod, and has edited *The Penguin Book of Australian Ballads.*

COMMONWEALTH VOLUMES

British East Africa *by Colin T. Leys*
Canada *by Frank Underhill*
Central Africa *by Prosser Gifford*
Ceylon *by S. Arasaratnam* (Published 1964)
Ghana and Nigeria *by John Flint*
Great Britain *by Norman Cantor*
India *by Stanley Wolpert* (Published 1965)
Malaysia *by John Bastin*
New Zealand *by William J. Cameron* (Published 1965)
Sierre Leone and Liberia *by Christopher Fyfe*
The West Indian Islands *by D. A. G. Waddell*

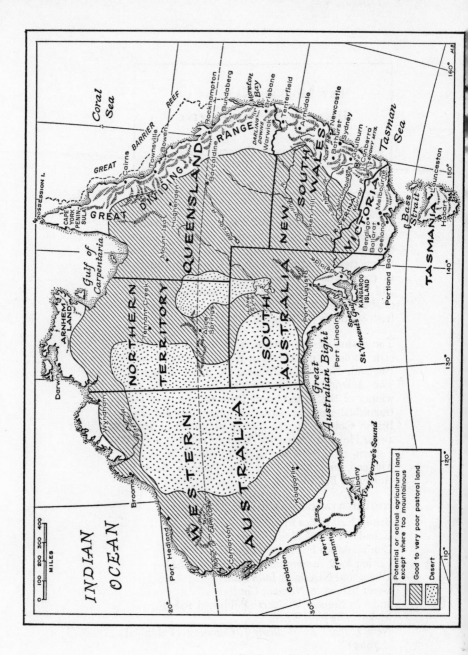

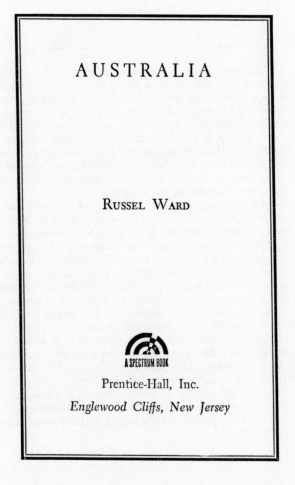

AUSTRALIA

RUSSEL WARD

A SPECTRUM BOOK

Prentice-Hall, Inc.

Englewood Cliffs, New Jersey

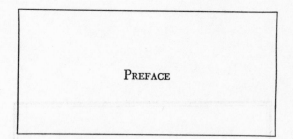

PREFACE

This book seeks to stress those elements in Australian history which have been most influential in giving the inhabitants of the country a sense of their own distinctive identity, and so in making a new nation. For, Australia is a sovereign national state as well as very much a part of the British Commonwealth, and though Australians achieved their sense of nationhood largely by emphasizing the differences between their way of life and that of the mother-country, these differences were after all rather slight in most ways. Few Australians now feel any sense of contradiction between their nationality and their close association with Great Britain and other countries of the Commonwealth.

Apart from its intrinsic interest, the history of Australia may be found particularly instructive by students of the development of "new countries" of European overseas settlement. It provides what economists might call a "model" of the course such development may take when the relationship between the developing colony and the mother-country is disturbed hardly at all by other factors. For throughout its formative period Australia was influenced very little by fear of powerful neighbors, by any considerable number of foreign immigrants, or even by a warlike or numerous aboriginal race. It is doubtful whether any nation ever had so few really intractable problems to cope with or has been left so alone, yet so protected from outside interference, while feeling its way forward to its own identity.

For helpful advice and criticism in preparing the manuscript I am indebted to my colleague Mr. John Robertson; and to honor and postgraduate students, especially Messrs. J. C. Caldwell, P. Cady, N. D. Green, Ken Macnab, J. F. Mason, M. V. Moore, and G. A. Price, for permission to use their research theses. My debt to other Australian historians is indicated, but not adequately acknowledged, in the footnotes and the list of suggested readings.

R.W.

Australia is a land of geographical superlatives which, despite great sweeps of distance and a strategic location off the southern shores of Southeast Asia, has remained historically mute for most Americans. The only nation which is a continent, one of the oldest and most staunch members of the Commonwealth of Nations, an inheritor of the traditions of the British Empire, Australia is today an expanding country which alone among the independent nations of the South Pacific is assuming the role of a middle power. But in all these contexts—Commonwealth, imperial, Southeast Asian, and Pacific—Australia remains little known or understood. Popularly believed to be a nation of empty wastes and fleece-lined hills, Australia actually is one of the most urbanized countries on earth and by some margin the most industrialized in the Southern Hemisphere. Thought by many to be similar to the United States, the Commonwealth of Australia is in fact a land rather unlike those of North America, for its history, and the institutions developed through that history, took a different path. It is this path which Russel Ward traces for us here.

Professor Ward's earlier contributions to Australian history have been controversial and far-reaching. *The Australian Legend*, published in 1958, in particular helped to give a new direction to Australian historiography, and it frequently has been compared to Henry Nash Smith's *Virgin Land*, a work of singular significance to the literary and cultural history of the United States. Today, for the first time, Australian historians are engaged in root-and-branch reassessments of their subject which frequently have created new controversies that have reached far beyond academic halls.

In one sense Professor Ward may be thought to represent the earlier school of historians against whom the recent revolt is directed, for he places heavy emphasis, as they did, on the influence of the "outback," on the character of the labor movement, and on the function of a working-men's ethos. But he also speaks for the recent trends in Australian historical writing, taking some of his techniques and insights from the discipline of American Studies, combining literature, the social sciences, and history (itself recognized to be a humanity) in one inquiry. He is interested in the nature of the Australian character, in the Australian self-image, and in the Australian value system. He writes as a self-conscious and committed Australian, and he speaks here of those subjects which an Australian considers important, writing in the authentic cadences of his nation. He speaks directly to his countrymen as well, for Professor Ward's analysis of Australian history brings together for the first time many of the suggestions he has made only by implication elsewhere. Americans and Australians alike will learn much from his particular historical perspective; that both may on occasion be moved to dispute him testifies to the vitality of his approach.

Robin W. Winks
Series Editor

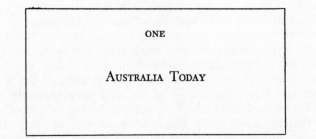

ONE

AUSTRALIA TODAY

If we except Antarctica, the Australian continent was probably the last to be occupied by man and certainly the last to be discovered by civilized people. There is evidence to suggest, though not to prove, that in the early fifteenth century a Chinese fleet touched on the northern coastline at the present site of Darwin.[1] In the sixteenth century Portuguese sailors may have sighted the shoreline. Between 1606 and the third quarter of the seventeenth century Abel Tasman and other Dutch navigators roughly charted the coast from Cape York to the head of the Great Australian Bight, and the southern coast of Tasmania, but the more fertile and relatively well-watered eastern shores remained unknown until their discovery in 1770 by the Englishman, James Cook. Since then a progressive, prosperous, democratic nation has been built in what was a remote and nearly empty wilderness. Today Australia's influence—and responsibilities—are probably greater than those of any other country in the southern hemisphere, though most people, including most Australians, are only beginning to be aware of what has happened.

In 1912 Edwin E. Slossom, a United States traveler, visited the site of Canberra, which had just been chosen as the new nation's capital. He wrote:

I naturally expected to find the people highly elated over the selection of their country as the best place in Australia for the federal capital. . . . But quite the contrary. I have seen a thousand times more excitement over the location of a Kansas courthouse. The prevalent spirit of the country is pessimism, spiced with contempt and cooled with indifference.[2]

This report underlines an attitude to life which observers have long thought to be peculiarly characteristic of, though by no means pecul-

[1] C. P. Fitzgerald, "A Chinese Discovery of Australia?," in *Australia Writes*, ed. T. Inglis Moore (Melbourne, 1953).
[2] Lionel Wigmore, *The Long View* (Melbourne, 1963), p. 49.

iar to, Australians. It also suggests how comparatively recent, and how influential, has been Australia's "frontier" experience.

We have emphasized this attitude because he who would understand the history of a nation may wisely study first those things which differentiate it from others, rather than those things which many nations, or even all human beings, hold in common. If this were not so, one who knew the history of his own country would already understand the histories of others, without having to go to the trouble of thinking about them. This is not to suggest, of course, that we need study nothing else but the singular differentiating features in a nation's history. Still less is it to imply that all Australians are, or ever have been, tough and sardonic characters such as those noticed by Mr. Slossom. It is merely to note that most Australians, at any rate until recently, have tended to admire the romanticized national self-image of the hard-bitten yet easy-going leveler; while the more cultivated minority, while often joining with most visitors to damn the stereotype, have yet recognized the likeness just as clearly. In what follows, then, while giving a general outline of Australian history, we shall concentrate especially on the causes of what is peculiar to, or characteristic of, the country.

Language and Style

What is Australia like today? As implied above, it is, like the United States or New Zealand, a new nation whose people, with their ideas and institutions, have been transplanted from Europe and especially from the British Isles during the last few hundred years. A well-traveled French, Russian, or Japanese visitor would quickly realize that he was moving in just another Anglo-Saxon democracy like Canada or Britain itself. A North American visitor, without any prior knowledge of Australia, would come to the same conclusion even more rapidly. He would probably land in Sydney and, there especially, he would be likely to feel more at home than anywhere else on earth outside his own continent. With a population now approaching 2,500,000, and built round a magnificent harbor with some 300 miles of shoreline, the largest city in Australia might remind our North American visitor of San Francisco. There, as throughout the country, he would find himself among people whose appearance and whose ways of eating, drinking, dressing, and talking are very much like his own. Not identical with his own, however. Perhaps the first difference to strike him would be the strange-sounding English spoken by Australians. If he were curious enough to follow up this clue he might learn a great deal more about Australia than merely the peculiarities of the local pronunciation of English, and the local derivation of the many colloquialisms not used elsewhere. For a hundred years and more most visitors have concurred in deploring the Australian accent. They complain that it is distressingly flat and nasal. Often it is compared, or even held to be identical with, the "Cockney" accent of working-class Londoners. But in matters of pronunciation beauty resides largely in the ear of the listener. Most people everywhere find natural, and hence euphonious, that mode of speech which they employ themselves. So most, though not all, Australians find standard Southern English speech insufferably high-pitched, bleating, and affected. Majority Australian speech is in fact more like Cockney than it is like the speech of Oxford or Lancashire or Toronto or New Orleans; and this kinship derives originally from the disproportionately large numbers of London thieves and pickpockets who came to Australia in the early days, at the expense of the British Government, as convicts. Vowels tend to be pronounced in the same closed way, so that "fight" approximates "foight" and "mate," "mite." On the other hand, Australian speech has none of the up-and-down lilt of Cockney. It is usually delivered slowly in a flat monotone. Brian Fitzpatrick, a distinguished Australian historian, has summed the matter up thus:

> But perhaps the majority (i.e. male) Australian approach to articulation is best indicated by a generalization: utterance is better not done at all; but, if it is done, when it is done, it were well it were slowly and flatly and expressionlessly, to betoken that the subject, any subject, is hardly worth talking about.[3]

The nature of Australian speech points to two other salient features of Australian life—the relatively high degree of class-consciousness coexisting with the generally democratic tone of society, and the lack of any marked regional or sectional differences. Transient or superficial observers have often given the impression that the broadest kind of Australian speech is the sole and universal one—as though all American accents were to be equated with that of the Bronx. Thus Professor Denis Brogan of Oxford wrote after his visit in 1958: "To hear an intelligent, critical, sardonic conversation in an accent which, in England, one associates with near-illiteracy, is a startling experience." It is true, of course, that there are general characteristics of Australian pronunciation, just as there are general characteristics of North American pronunciation, which distinguish each unmistakably from B.B.C. or standard Southern English: but there are also marked

[3] *The Australian Commonwealth* (Melbourne, 1956), p. 28.

differences within each. In North America these differences tend to be regional in character; in Australia they tend, though not at all rigidly, to be social. Professor A. G. Mitchell has demonstrated the existence of two ubiquitous kinds of pronunciation which he designates Broad Australian and Educated Australian. The latter employs relatively open vowel sounds, though it tends to be almost as flat and monotonous in pitch as the former. It is more readily comprehensible to most visitors and is nearer to B.B.C. or even to "Harvard English." On the whole, Educated Australian, as its name implies, is heard among the better educated sections of the community and Broad Australian among "the masses"; but the two modes of pronunciation shade into each other so that no clear dividing line can be drawn, and there are quite a few judges, distinguished writers, and cabinet ministers (of both the Labor and anti-Labor parties) who speak Broad Australian, just as there are some wharf laborers and taxi drivers who speak Educated Australian. This pronunciation pattern reflects the state of society described by an acute English visitor in 1903:

> It is sometimes said that in Australia there are no class distinctions. It would probably be truer to say that in no country in the world are there such strong class distinctions in proportion to the actual amount of difference between the "classes." . . . The "classes" collectively distrust and fear the "masses" collectively far more than is the case at home. . . . Individually, it is true, relations are for the most part amicable enough between capitalists and workmen; and the lack of deference in the tone of the employees, their employers, being unable to resent, have grown to tolerate, and even perhaps in some cases secretly rather to like. . . .[4]

This muted and nonviolent, but persistent, class antagonism has become possibly less marked over the years, but speech habits reflect the fact that it still exists.

They reflect too the fact of the *sameness* of Australia. Philologists have so far failed to find any significant regional differences whatever in Australian pronunciation. One can immediately tell roughly where a speaker's voice belongs in the pronunciation spectrum ranging from very Broad to self-consciously Educated Australian but, after listening for an hour, no one can say whether the speaker comes from Perth or Cairns, Melbourne or Alice Springs. Uniformity of pronunciation is largely a result of the fact that Australians, probably even more than Americans, migrate freely and frequently from state to state and have always done so; but relatively great uniformity extends also to the landscape and the land itself. All this is summed up evocatively in

[4] Percy F. Rowland, *The New Nation* (London, 1903), pp. 119 f.

one of A. D. Hope's poems, *Australia*—the sameness of both the desert inland and the only comparatively less dry coastal areas, and the enduring astringency with which Australians tend to regard themselves and the universe:

> A nation of trees, drab green and desolate grey
> In the field uniform of modern wars
> Darkens her hills, those endless, outstretched paws
> Of sphinx demolished or stone lion worn away.
>
> They call her a young country, but they lie:
> She is the last of lands, the emptiest,
> A woman beyond her change of life, a breast
> Still tender but within the womb is dry.
>
> Without songs, architecture, history:
> The emotions and superstitions of younger lands.
> Her rivers of water drawn among inland sands
> The river of her immense stupidity
>
> Floods her monotonous tribes from Cairns to Perth.
> In them at last the ultimate men arrive
> Whose boast is not: "we live" but "we survive"
> A type who will inhabit the dying earth.
>
> And her five cities, like five teeming sores
> Each drains her, a vast parasite robber-state
> Where second-hand Europeans pullulate
> Timidly on the edge of alien shores.[5]

But as R. M. Crawford has written, "Satire is the weapon of the idealist once bitten but twice shy." [6] Because his experience has taught him to shun high-flown notions and to endure, the Australian still hopes that something of real value may spring from his assimilation to his dry land. Hope's poem ends:

> Yet there are some like me turn gladly home
> From the lush jungle of modern thought, to find
> The Arabian desert of the human mind,
> Hoping, if still from deserts the prophets come,
>
> Such savage and scarlet as no green hills dare
> Springs in that waste, some spirit which escapes
> The learned doubt, the chatter of cultured apes
> Which is called civilisation over there.

[5] *Modern Australian Poetry*, ed. H. M. Green (Melbourne, 1946).
[6] *An Australian Perspective* (Madison, 1960), p. 75.

Land and People

The poem reminds us also of the extent to which the vast interior of the continent—where few of them ever lived—has tended to dominate the imagination of Australians. A similar process took place in the United States during the nineteenth century while "the West was won." It is true that, relatively, many more Americans live in the interior, far from sophisticated Boston, New York, Philadelphia, and Europe; but on the other hand Sydney, Melbourne, Brisbane, Adelaide, and Perth are themselves so much more remote from older centers of European civilization. Since World War Two this imaginative inwardness, and the tendency toward a quasipolitical isolationism which it nourished, has weakened very noticeably in Australia as in America. There are many aspects of Australia which an American finds familiar.

The two countries are similar, if we exclude Alaska, in area and shape. In both the first European settlements were made on the eastern seaboard. In the United States some of these pioneering villages were to become great cities. In Australia the first settlements also grew to greatness and remain today as the only real centers of commerce, manufacture, and culture. In both countries settlement was at first confined to the eastern coastal plain which is, however, in Australia less well-watered, narrower, and provided with fewer natural harbors than its American counterpart. In both countries, too, the eastern coastal plain is backed by a more or less continuous range of mountains. Australia's Great Dividing Range is, for the most part, not much loftier than the Alleghenies, though in many places the eastern escarpment of "the Great Divide" is steeper and much more difficult to cross. West of the range the land falls away gradually to seemingly endless plains as in North America, but here the geographical parallel breaks down. Australia's inland is vastly drier and hotter than America's. For perhaps 200 miles west of the watershed there is, in favored districts, enough rainfall to make modern, large-scale agriculture possible. Beyond this belt there is another, up to 500 miles or so wide, which supports a sparse occupation by pastoralists who graze sheep for the most part, though cattle predominate in the northern areas. Australia's greatest river system, that of the Murray-Darling, bears little resemblance to that of the Mississippi-Missouri. The former is only faintly comparable with the latter in extent, while in fertility and aridity it is much more like the lower basin of the Rio Grande. For Australia has no high mountain chain like the Rockies to the westward of the land-mass. Beyond the last drought-stricken sheep-stations (ranches) some 600 miles from the eastern coast, the whole country is uninhabited for about 1,500 miles until a few stock-stations appear again near the flat and still almost rainless western coast. Here and there in this vast expanse a chain of low hills may attract the hardy miner or prospector, or another range may trap enough rainfall to provide occasional surface water for a few lonely graziers to eke out an existence, if hardly a living. Another Australian poet, James McAuley, thus sums up his country's geography and his countrymen's attitude to it. Jonathan Swift's Gulliver, who discovered Lilliput "north-west of Van Diemen's Land, in latitude 30° S," is imagined reporting to his patron:

> The place, my lord, is much like Gideon's fleece
> The second time he laid it on the ground;
> For by the will of God it has remained
> Bone-dry itself, with water all around.
>
> Yet, as a wheel that's driven in the ruts
> It has a wet rim where the people clot
> Like mud; and though they praise the inner spaces,
> When asked to go themselves, they'd rather not.[7]

Naturally. Scattered sparsely over their vast and arid continent, and separated by vaster oceans from the original homeland whence their fathers came, Australians have long felt lonely; and though they have increasingly clotted together for comfort in the coastal cities, their inner loneliness persists. Loneliness is a striking element in the work of many leading contemporary painters like Russell Drysdale, William Dobell, Sidney Nolan, Arthur Boyd, and Bob Dickerson. So much so that in song and story the most highly prized Australian character trait is an easygoing friendliness, or "mateship," as it is called. In reaction to their loneliness, to the sundering distances and to the harshness of nature, men learned to help and trust each other. This is not to claim, of course, that Australians are in fact notably more altruistic than other people, but merely that they tend to value collective effort and mutual aid more highly than do, for example, Americans; just as they value less highly rugged individualism. Thus, though the virtues of "private enterprise" are much trumpeted at election times by the more conservative parties, collectivist and even socialist ideas and "paternalistic" legislation are relatively much more widespread in Australia, no matter what party is in power. The face of government is much more frequently seen than in the United States, and somewhat more so than in Canada. The federal post

[7] *Under Aldebaran* (Melbourne, 1946).

office, for instance, handles not only mail services but also the entire telegraph and telephone systems, and all railways are owned and run by governments.

Nowadays there is a strong reaction in Australian writing against the "Bush Legend" and the simple-minded cult of mateship. For instance the novels of the greatest contemporary Australian writer, Patrick White, imply that for him mateship is at best a superficial whistling-in-the-dark, and at worst a nauseating and hypocritical sham: but White's work, like that of A. D. Hope and James McAuley already referred to, underlines the loneliness—now of a much more subtle kind, however—that did so much to generate the earlier, simpler reaction. But we have written enough at present about the differences of shading and emphasis that, for the discerning, distinguish Australians from Americans. What of the more obvious similarities?

Both are preponderantly urbanized societies, though Australia is relatively more urbanized than the United States, or indeed than any other country in the world: at least if we define "urban" as living in cities of more than 200,000 people. Of her 11,500,000, half live within a radius of 100 miles of her two major cities, Sydney and Melbourne. Another quarter live in or very near the remaining state capitals, Adelaide, Brisbane, Perth, and Hobart. North Americans sometimes find Australian cities a little old-fashioned or British in atmosphere, but all would probably agree with Professor Joseph Jones of the University of Texas about the basic similarity between the two countries. Jones wrote:

Perth is two days from Johannesburg by plane, in the same hemisphere but in a different century. Or so it seemed to me, when late in 1960 after nine months in South Africa I landed there. Had there been two weeks at sea, the contrast might not have been so dramatic; as it was, I felt I was home already. During the months to follow, differences became apparent. But upon final departure—by ship this time, from Cairns, at the north-east corner, directly opposite where I came in— it was still difficult to believe that I was leaving foreign soil.[8]

In the broadest sense Australians and Americans share the language, culture, traditions, and manners common to the great capitalist democracies of the English-speaking world. About a quarter of the population describe themselves in census returns as Catholics, about a third as adherents of the Church of England, and most of the remainder as subscribing to Methodist, Presbyterian, or other Protestant faiths. About 10 per cent profess no religious belief. Public education

[8] "Image of Australia," in *Texas Quarterly* (Austin), Vol. 2, Summer 1962, p. 7.

is primarily the business of state governments—not, as in Britain and America, of local authorities. The state governments provide separate, though similar, fairly highly centralized primary and secondary school systems. Education is free for all children whose parents care to send them to state schools, and school attendance, in most states up to the age of at least fifteen, is compulsory. The Roman Catholic Church, holding that its members cannot conscientiously send their children to the secular state schools, maintains a separate network of schools staffed mainly by nuns and teaching brothers. The great majority of Catholic children attend these church schools, which charge relatively low fees. The major Protestant churches maintain a very much smaller number of more or less fashionable schools which are modeled largely on the "great public schools" of England and which charge high fees. Only a small proportion of children, drawn for the most part from well-to-do, middle-class families, attend these schools which, nevertheless, have long exercised a moderating influence on the marked leveling tendencies in Australian society. Their influence is less strong than that of similar schools in Britain, but stronger than that of "preparatory schools" and other such private institutions in the United States and Canada.

Government and Politics

Australian political institutions are also, in most ways, similar to those of America, even down to perennial rumors of corruption in city politics, especially in the eastern capitals. Constitutionally, of course, the head of state is an hereditary monarch and not an elected president. Elizabeth II is queen of Australia as well as of Great Britain, and loyalty to the Crown is a sentiment deeply if unostentatiously felt by most Australians. But the governor-general and the state governors, who carry out the sovereign's constitutional functions, are appointed on the recommendation of the elected governments. Distinguished Englishmen are usually nominated to these vice-regal posts by Liberal governments and Australians by Labor governments, for conservatives have always tended to stress common British imperial loyalty and those whose politics are to the left of center have tended to stress instead local Australian nationalist sentiment. Again this is a matter of shading and emphasis. Most Australians find the two kinds of loyalty not at all incompatible, but rather complementary.

Like the United States Australia is, theoretically, not a unitary nation but a federation of states, though in both countries the federal government constantly acquires relatively more and more prestige. The six Australian states, in descending order of population, development of secondary industries, and over-all production, are New South Wales, Victoria, Queensland, South Australia, Western Australia, and Tasmania. Each state except Queensland, which abolished its upper house in 1922, has a bicameral legislature. In all the lower house (Legislative Assembly) is elected by universal adult franchise, and voting is compulsory. In this last provision for the obligatory exercise of citizenship some have seen a reflection of the Australian tendency to emphasize the collectivist rather than the individualist aspects of democracy. In some states the upper house (Legislative Council) is still elected on a slightly restricted franchise (S. A., Tas., and W. A.), or indirectly (N. S. W.), but all the upper houses, with decreasing prestige, can usually exercise only marginal influence on legislation. After an election the leader of the successful party in the lower house is commissioned by the state governor as premier. If Labor candidates have obtained a majority of the seats they—all Labor members of both houses "in caucus"—elect from their own number the cabinet ministers who are then assigned portfolios by the premier. If the anti-Labor parties have won the election, the majority party leader and premier both chooses his own ministers and allots portfolios among them. New elections must be held every three years, but of course Parliament may be dissolved at any time if the government loses the confidence of the lower house.

Each state has its own police force and judicial system, but there are no locally controlled city or district police forces. Judges, magistrates, and other public officials are, generally speaking, appointed for life as in other British Commonwealth countries, and are not subject to dismissal when there is a change of government. In theory, and to a perhaps surprising degree in practice, this results in the impartial and nonpolitical exercise of their powers by public officials; even though many of them are appointed on the recommendation—practically the nomination—of the party in power.

As in America the state governments are theoretically sovereign, retaining all "residual" or unspecified powers. In practice they tend to be occupied quite largely with fields that are more often the concern of district and municipal governing bodies in Great Britain and North America. The largest slice of every state budget is spent, for example, on education. Railways and some other forms of public transport are also a major concern of the states. This condition of affairs did not spring initially from any doctrinaire socialist or collectivist theories. Rather such tendencies toward "leaning on the government" and toward centralization were imposed by the conditions of Australian geography and history. In a vast country where the population density is still only about three persons to the square mile railways, however essential for development, cannot be made to pay. Businessmen themselves, therefore, were prominent among those who early demanded that governments shoulder the burden. The arrangement has some advantages for, while looking to his governments for help and comfort, the Australian likes at the same time to abuse them for incompetence. Governments can be heartily damned because the railways constantly drain the public purse and, more cogently, because lack of official foresight long ago saddled the country with three different railway gauges—4 foot 8½ inches in New South Wales and on some Commonwealth lines, 5 foot 3 inches in Victoria and some parts of South Australia, 3 foot 6 inches in other parts of South Australia and in Western Australia, Queensland, and Tasmania. Until recently this meant that goods sent by rail from Brisbane to Perth had to be transshipped five times en route. Duplication of gauges on a few key trunk lines has now reduced these transshipment points to three.

The federal government exercises certain specific powers which are obviously of general national concern: for example power over external affairs, immigration and emigration, trade and customs, posts and telegraphs, defense. It also administers underdeveloped and dependent areas like the Northern Territory and Papua-New Guinea. Citizens of the Australian Capital Territory in which Canberra is situated can, in some respects, have their cake and eat it too. While enjoying some special amenities such as unusually fine public school buildings and grounds paid for from buoyant federal revenues, they may claim to be second-class citizens and so doubly damn the government: for, as with the citizens of the Northern Territory, their elected member may speak but not vote in the lower house except on matters of purely local concern.

In the federal legislature the lower house is known as the House of Representatives and the upper as the Senate. Members of both houses are elected by universal adult franchise. In the lower house representation is on a population basis. That is to say, each of its 124 members (except for the two Northern Territory and Capital Territory spokesmen) represents an electorate of approximately equal population— about 80,000 in 1960—so that New South Wales has nearly fifty representatives in the lower house, while Western Australia has only nine and Tasmania five. In the upper house senators represent, theoretically as in America, state interests. The people of each state, conceived as a single electorate, choose ten senators, each of whom is elected for a six-year term so as to give some continuity to Parliament. Thus at each federal election, normally held every three years, five senators are chosen by the people of each state to replace the five whose six-year term of office has expired. In practice, however, divisions and groupings in the Senate are nearly always along purely party lines, as in the lower house. The cry of state rights may be heard nearly as often in one chamber as in the other and from politicians of all parties. People criticize "the old men in the Senate." Nevertheless, partly because of the completely democratic franchise on which it is elected, this chamber possesses considerably more power and prestige than do any of the state upper houses.

Australia enjoys, or suffers, a two-party system of government very similar indeed to that of Great Britain and quite like that of the United States in many respects but not in others. Historians, when speaking in general terms, are usually constrained to refer to the Labor and anti-Labor parties because the latter group has changed its name, if not its basic policy, so often. Since the separate colonies federated in 1901 the more conservative of the two main parties has styled itself, in turn, Fusionist, Liberal, Nationalist, United Australia Party (U. A. P.), and then Liberal again. If words mean anything there is no question but that this party is, in Australian terms, the more conservative of the two major political groups: yet, if one compares its policies and performance with those of conservative parties in Great Britain and still more in North America, it may legitimately be called Liberal—at least in many aspects of its domestic, if not so much of its foreign, policies. Why the changes of name? Probably because in Australia the word "conservative" carries enough anti-nationalist and anti-democratic overtones to make it unacceptable as a label to political realists. Even in the second half of the last century, before stable party groupings formed in the colonial parliaments, almost every politician, including the most conservative among them, described himself on the hustings as a "liberal."

What of the Labor Party? Again, if words mean anything, it is unquestionably the more radical (in the common sense of "leftist") of the two groups. Is it a socialist party? Socialism as the party's policy—"socialization of industry, production, distribution, and exchange"—tends to be played up by party speakers before some Labor League and most trade-union audiences, and played down or even denied during election campaigns. The Labor Party claims to stand for the national interests of the whole Australian people because it is thought to stand first for the interests of the wage-earning majority. The Liberal Party claims to stand for the best interests of the whole people because it claims to eschew "class interests" of any kind. Naturally its political opponents charge that it really stands primarily for business interests, just as Labor's opponents charge that Labor really stands for sectional working-class interests to the detriment of the national life as a whole. In practice, as opposed to propaganda, there is a great deal less difference between the performances of the two parties in office than an American, accustomed to the ins and outs of two parties both firmly committed to the virtues of free enterprise, might expect. A student of American politics, seeking therein analogies to help him grasp the rudiments of the Australian political scene, will not be far wrong if he proceeds thus. First compare the Liberal Party with the Republicans and the Labor Party with the Democrats, but at the same time remember that the whole political spectrum must be shifted considerably to the left. Second, remember that the Labor Party is not unlike what the Democratic Party would be if shorn of its conservative "Dixiecrat" wing.

As in America the two major parties compete for office in both state and federal politics, but there is a third party of some real significance in Australia—the Country Party. Since farmers and other country-dwellers comprise only an increasingly small minority of the population, and since the Country Party, as its name proclaims, stands for sectional primary producer interests, this group seems condemned to permanent opposition or to dependent alliance with one of the two major national parties. In the past some Country Party members have been temperamentally more conservative than many Liberals, and in the federal Parliament for the last half century or so the Liberals have held office only at the price of entering into an apparently permanent alliance with the Country Party members. Though Labor supporters are apt to regard the Country Party as merely a wing, often the conservative wing, of the Liberal Party, the Liberal–Country Party alliance has not been maintained without considerable internal strain; for while both major parties are firmly committed to a policy of protection for secondary industries, the man on the land, while naturally ever ready to seek protection for his own products, still hankers after cheap imported machinery and other consumer goods. The federal pattern of practical dependence on the Liberal Party is reproduced in most of the state parliaments, though in South Australia the two parties have long been one even in a formal sense under the style of the Liberal–Country League, and in Victoria for some years the Country Party held power as a minority government with the support of the Labor Party. In Queensland, where relatively many more people live in the bush than in any other state, the Country Party for some years from 1960 held the premiership and the majority of seats in a Country–Liberal Party coalition government.

One other feature of Australian political life must be noted, if only because it has been so much canvassed during recent years.

About 25 per cent of Australians are Roman Catholics, preponderantly of Irish descent. For reasons that will be discussed later, citizens of Catholic faith and Irish ancestry were always disproportionately numerous—though of late years decreasingly so—among wage-earners. Naturally they tend to support the Labor Party and, though of course many Catholics vote for other parties, about half of all Labor members of Parliament are Catholics, while a Catholic Liberal or Country Party member is something of a rarity. Thus Labor must contain peaceably within itself this sectarian difference and potential source of strife, which scarcely troubles its opponents. When, as for a decade or more following 1954, it fails to do so, the Labor Party is apt to see more than usual of the opposition benches.

We have dealt with the political scene at some length to show that, though it exhibits important differences, it is on the whole basically familiar, or at least readily comprehensible, to other English-speaking peoples. The same may be said of most other aspects of Australian life. Indeed many travelers, in both the last century and this, have seen Australian society as little more than an amalgam of contending British and American influences. This is true but by no means the whole truth. What then about Australian life is specifically different from British and American life?

Attitudes and Problems

In material things the differences are most inconsiderable, though perhaps also most immediately obvious. Streets, houses, office blocks, movie houses, service stations, airports, and stores are on the whole readily interchangeable with their British or American equivalents; although all such things give the impression of being rather more glossy and "modern" than in Britain, rather less so than in the United States. On the other hand, ordinary dwelling houses in Australia differ markedly from both their British and North American counterparts, and not at all by the adoption of a style intermediate between the other two. To Australian eyes British and North American houses look like diminutive boxes or dolls' houses. It is not that they are in fact smaller (though they usually are in Britain), but that they seem to be so because of the compact appearance that comes from their having two stories. Australian private homes almost always have only one story and are roofed with galvanized iron, less often with tiles. Very often they have one or more outside verandas or terraces attached. Though the actual floor space of an Australian home is probably, on the average, less than that of an American or Canadian one, the Australian house sprawls untidily and looks bigger because it covers much more ground.

Social institutions, as we have seen in the case of the political system, differ rather more than do material objects from their overseas equivalents, though it may take the visitor longer to realize this. Let us take for example the institution of tipping. Relatively speaking, it hardly exists in Australia. Nothing so disturbs the Australian abroad for the first time as does the need to get used to it. What troubles him is not the expense of tipping, but the necessity of participating in a relationship between human beings which seems to him to assume the existence of a basic inequality between them. Of course there are certain well-defined areas in Australian life where tipping is normal practice. Everyone knows that porters at railway and shipping (though not airways) terminals earn their living thus; but the total area of living in which tipping is expected in Australia (and New Zealand) is minute compared with that in any other country whatever. Yet a visitor from abroad, accustomed to tipping waitresses at every meal, might not realize that things were in the least different in this respect in Australia if he spent all his time in fashionable city hotels much frequented by overseas travelers.

The major differences, however, are probably not material or institutional, but mental and emotional. That sounds ridiculous and it would be stupid to overstress these differences, just as it would be to minimize them, as some misguidedly do in a commendable effort to promote friendship between English-speaking peoples. Psychology has long since shown that human beings everywhere are motivated by the same basic instincts, and an American psychologist who migrated to Australia would probably find less environmentally caused modification of his ideas necessary than if he settled anywhere else on earth, except perhaps in Canada. Nevertheless, the longer he lived in Australia, the greater would he find the differences between the two peoples in mental style and attitudes. The Australian tends to be more easy-going, cooperative, and enduring, less ebullient, competitive, and hard-driving than the American, though both alike are so much more informal and "democratic" in manner than the Englishman.

Of course there are many efficient, ambitious, and energetic Australians just as there are some lethargic Americans. All such differences in outlook are differences in emphasis and tendency and none, in the nature of things, begins to be absolute. The most we can say by way of generalization is that, on the average, Australians admire individualist virtues less, and collectivist ones more, than do Americans. In situations where an American might say "Get up and go!," an Australian is more likely to say "Aw. We'll give it a go," and there is a world of difference between the psychological overtones carried by the two phrases. The first implies abounding energy and determination to succeed. The second implies off-hand willingness to take a sporting chance: success or failure are in the lap of the gods and the outcome doesn't matter all *that* much anyway. Where Americans tend to admire the man who fights his way to the top in the face of material and human obstacles, Australians tend to admire rather the "battler"—the common man who battles on, is loyal to his mates, but never achieves success except by chance and then he should have the grace to be a little embarrassed by it. Australians are apt to suspect the *bona-fides* of a successful man just *because* he is successful. By most Australians the achievement of fame or riches is, in itself, more likely to be taken as *prima facie* evidence of unusually great greed, guile, or luck than of unusually great capacity. Hence springs, as distinguished Australians are wont to complain almost as often as foreign observers, the unusually widespread delight that Australians feel in taking down the mighty from their seats—a pastime known in the vernacular as "knocking."

Freedom, to an American, tends to mean freedom to be independent of others, to be different. To an Australian, the equally unthought-of meaning of the word tends to be freedom to combine with others for the collective good, even freedom to conform to group patterns—which, however, differ subtly from group patterns elsewhere. Thus, in political and other spheres, collectivist institutions and assumptions are much more widely tolerated, if not accepted, in Australia than in the United States. Relative to total populations and, even more strikingly, relative to what might be expected from the comparative degree of industrialization in the two countries, trade unions have always been very much more powerful in Australia. Administration is more centralized and government controls more far-reaching. Both state and federal courts for the arbitration of industrial disputes between employers and employees have long been established. To American eyes, people tend to be more concerned than they should be with job security and less with competitive endeavor. Though many Australians denounce these tendencies as balefully as any American Babbit, they are themselves influenced by them. In the professional ranks of the universities and the civil services, for example, promotion is governed much more by seniority rules and much less by achievement or "merit" than would be acceptable in the United States; and the most conservative Australian advocates of free competition naturally tend to be less messianic when conditions of employment in their own fields of work are being discussed. Life in short tends to be more relaxed in Australia, and Australians contemplate it in a more fatalistic, less earnest spirit.

Up until the end of the First World War the greatest Australian novel was Joseph Furphy's *Such Is Life*. It begins with the rapturous words, "Unemployed at last!"—and ends with the self-mocking sentences:

> Such is life my fellow-mummers—just like a poor player, that bluffs and feints his hour upon the stage, and then cheapens down to mere nonentity. But let me not hear any small witticism to the further effect that its story is a tale told by a vulgarian, full of slang and blanky, signifying—nothing.

Where, as R. K. Merton and others have shown, American popular literature and mythology reflect the "Log Cabin to White House" theme, their Australian counterparts reflect instead a theme which might be styled "Bark-hut or shearing-shed to the shanty [American, *saloon*], and back again." Most Australians still prize leisure above riches or "success."

The "still" introduces another qualification. We have stressed above that these differences in outlook, though important, are marginal and not absolute in nature. The second qualification is that they are probably decreasing. Today it would be possible for an intelligent North American visitor to spend a few weeks (though probably not months) in Australian business or other middle-class circles, especially in the great cities, without noticing the existence of some of the differences we have been discussing. Since World War Two Australia, like most other parts of the world, has been increasingly strongly influenced by American—or "modern," cosmopolitan—attitudes: but for reasons which have deep roots in her history, Australia's entry into the mainstream of world events has been much more sudden than that of most other Western nations. A recent history of the country was revealingly subtitled *The Quiet Continent*.[9] For many generations an extraordinarily homogeneous group of British people, transplanted to an isolated but extensive corner of the earth, quietly adapted themselves to it and developed in the process their own way of life. No warlike neighbors disputed their occupation of the continent, and no civil tumults seriously disturbed their steady growth into nationhood. Such tranquil, uninterrupted development depended upon the worldwide power of their indulgent, if sometimes irritating, mother country: but Australians generally took their incredibly fortunate situation for granted as part of the nature of the universe—until it disappeared with the Second World War. Then rather suddenly they had to defend themselves, make their own decisions on matters of national life or death, and make their own

---

[9] Douglas Pike, *Australia: the Quiet Continent* (London, 1962).

arrangements with other countries, including Asian countries long ignored or contemned but no longer distant or impotent. At the same time, Australian industry reached the "takeoff" point, and for the first time large numbers of non-British immigrants were added to the population. Living Australians face much greater opportunities, perils, and complexities than any known to their ancestors. They are probably changing more rapidly accordingly, and this modification of traditional ways is welcomed and promoted by some Australians just as it is opposed and deplored by others: though the great majority, like people everywhere, "are what they are" without thinking much about what that is, or what it is becoming.

The characteristic Australian attitudes sketched above, needless to say, are not carried in the blood, nor are they mystical emanations from the Southern Cross or from the aromatic leaves of the ubiquitous gum trees. They result from the nation's historical experience. In the following chapters we shall outline the nature of this experience, paying particular and even disproportionate attention to those aspects of it which tended to make the migrants diverge from accepted British attitudes and develop others of their own.

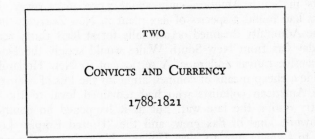

TWO

CONVICTS AND CURRENCY

1788-1821

By 1600 the Dutch East India Company had established itself firmly in Java. Six years later one of its vessels, the *Duyfken*, nosing about the archipelago for signs of gold and spices, discovered part of the eastern coastline of Cape York Peninsula. During the following century and a half, Dutch sailors charted roughly the position of the Australian coast from this point west and south to the head of the Great Australian Bight. There is no comparable length of shoreline in the world, outside the polar regions, so barren and uninviting. The Dutch showed little interest in it or in its few naked inhabitants, and no disposition at all to settle. The relatively well-watered eastern coast remained undiscovered until 1770. It was found and charted by Lieutenant James Cook, son of a Yorkshire laborer and noblest of circumnavigators. Cook had already helped Wolfe's army in Canada by charting parts of the St. Lawrence below Quebec, and was later to visit Canada's west coast. With the crew of his ship, *H. M. S. Endeavour*, and his illustrious passenger Joseph Banks, later to become for forty-one years president of Britain's leading scientific body, the Royal Society, Cook stayed for a week in Botany Bay about ten miles south of what is today the central part of Sydney. Four months later, on 21 August at Possession Island off Cape York, he formally claimed for his country all of eastern New Holland and named it New South Wales. Then the aboriginal inhabitants were left in peace for another eighteen years.

Convict Foundations

In 1788 the Australian nation was founded by and for Great Britain's surplus of convicted criminals, a fact which used to give many respectable Australians pain and which threatened a few with schizophrenia. It is true that some supporting reasons were advanced by contemporaries. British trade, it was hoped somewhat nebulously, would benefit from the establishment of the new settlement. It might prove a handy base from which to attack the Spanish settlements in South America—only about 7,000 miles away. Because Banks had found a species of flax plant in New Zealand, the Lords of the Admiralty dreamed occasionally for at least thirty years that one day flax from New South Wales would supply the Navy with inexpensive canvas and rope. A settlement in New Holland might provide a cheap means of compensating for the loss of their property those American colonists who had remained loyal to the mother country during the late war. But as it happened no commercially worthwhile kind of flax grew, and the "United Empire Loyalists" went to Canada, not to New Holland. Nevertheless, the victory of the thirteen American colonies in 1783 did much to bring about the foundation of Australia five years later. Before the War of Independence about a thousand British convicts had been shipped annually to the southern plantation settlements like Virginia. The number of convicts continued to increase during and after the war, but the independent Americans would no longer receive them. Some other abortive schemes, including a new settlement at some point on the African coast, were explored. Meanwhile more and more convicts were crammed into "temporary" accommodation in hulks moored in the Thames estuary and at Portsmouth. At last in 1787 the King's speech to Parliament announced that a plan had been formed "for transporting a number of convicts in order to remove the inconvenience which arose from the crowded state of the gaols." In May of the same year the First Fleet of eleven store-ships and transports set sail for Botany Bay. Its complement of something more than a thousand felons and their jailers disembarked in the virgin bush at Sydney Cove eight months later, on 26 January, 1788. It had been— for the period—a more than usually rapid and healthy voyage.

The first governor and commander-in-chief was Arthur Phillip, a sensible and, by contemporary standards, unusually humane naval captain. Almost alone among the first settlers, he foresaw the time when the miserable little jail might become a prosperous and civilized country: but the immediate struggle for survival taxed his strength to the limit. His human cargo had been dumped on the shore where Sydney now stands. About three-quarters of them were convicts— men, women, and children of whom many were aged or infirm, and nearly all unwilling to work, even if they had been bred to it. The remainder were mainly Marine Corps officers and men, sent out as a guard; but from the moment of landing the officers manifested a keen appreciation of their station in life. They refused to compromise what they regarded as their dignity by supervising the work of felons, except in the case of those who had been assigned to them personally as servants. Thus the best-behaved—or most sycophantic—convicts had to be made constables and placed in other positions of some responsibility. Most of the colonists were criminals from the slums of London and other great cities. There was hardly a gardener or farmer among them. Seeds refused to sprout in the alien soil, and for the first two years the infant colony was threatened with famine. Phillip placed his private stock of food in the communal store and decreed the same scale of rations for bond and free. The "starving time" had passed by the time he sailed for England in December, 1792, but the day when the colony would be self-supporting seemed almost as far off as ever.

Mild Aborigines

One difficulty that Australian pioneers—unlike those of North America, South Africa, and New Zealand—did not have to contend with was a warlike native race. The Australian aborigines are classed by most anthropologists as belonging to a fourth, or Australoid, group of mankind, probably more akin to Caucasoids than to Negroids. They were among the most primitive and peaceable peoples known to history. Without any kind of agriculture or domestic animal, except for the native wild dog, or dingo, sometimes tamed for hunting, and without even semipermanent dwellings, they lived entirely by food-gathering. Extended family groups, in loose contact with others of the same tribe, wandered about in search of edible plants and animals but always within their own traditionally defined tribal area. Their lives were strictly governed by immemorial custom and individuals who transgressed it were severely punished, often by death; but there is no evidence that they ever practiced the art of warfare as it is understood by more technologically advanced peoples. Nasty, brutish, and short though their lives were in so many ways, no aboriginal tribe ever seems to have conceived the notion of exterminating or enslaving another, or of stealing its collective property or territory. This is not to say that the aborigines did not sometimes reply in kind to violent or outrageous acts by the newcomers who occupied their lands; but their reaction was so sporadic and ineffectual that men seldom had to go armed on the Australian frontier. From Phillip's time until today Australian governments have had to be much more concerned with protecting the aborigines than with fighting them. Not that the rather formal efforts of the authorities in this direction were very successful. Australia's record in this sphere is no more creditable than that of the United States or of any other colony settled by Europeans during the eighteenth and nineteenth centuries, and less so than that of New Zealand. As the white settlers advanced inland to occupy new grazing land, tribe after tribe disintegrated when its traditional organization broke down and its hunting grounds were stolen. Whether the settlers treated the dark people brutally or humanely, none in the last century really understood their Stone Age culture. Some were hunted down and shot or poisoned like animals, but many more fell victims to the white man's diseases and to the spiritual sickness that resulted from the breakdown of their tribal life. At one time there were perhaps 300,000 aborigines in Australia. Today only about one sixth of that number of full-bloods survive, and most of these are detribalized and, at least to European eyes, demoralized.

The singularly unwarlike nature of the aboriginal race may well have had a lasting influence on Australian society. Though Australians pride themselves on their sporting prowess, though they are traditionally supposed to be unusually handy brawlers, and though in two world wars they have won an enviable reputation as first-class fighting troops, they have in fact been remarkably slow to kill *each other*. Leveling and loutishness spring naturally from frontier conditions, yet Australian brawls, strikes, and other uncivil tumults have almost always stopped short of manslaughter. Two criminals were probably put to death by lynch mobs on the Victorian goldfields in 1852. Some twenty-one gold diggers, soldiers, and policemen were killed in the Eureka rebellion, or riot, of 1854. A youth, Norman Brown, was shot dead by panicking policemen at Rothbury on the Hunter River coalfields during a strike in 1929 and three southern European immigrants were killed in race riots at Kalgoorlie in 1934, but it is not easy to find another case of this sort. Even professional criminals like the bushrangers (bandits) of the last century generally showed a greater reluctance to kill than their counterparts in other lands. Australians do not find it extraordinary that their classic novel of "frontier" experience, Furphy's *Such Is Life*, should contain no deeds of violence. In 1960 the whole country was deeply shocked by the *first* case of kidnapping in its history. It would be disingenuous to suppose that this relatively low level of violence in Australian life and history springs solely, or even mainly, from the nature of the aborigines and of the white settlers' relationship with them. Not less important were the absence of warlike neighbors and extraordinary homogeneity of the settlers' own national and cultural background. At any rate, until the last decade or so Australia had no troublesome neighbors like the Mexicans or Cubans and, among her own citizens, no substantial minority group like the people of French, German, Italian, or Negro descent in the United States. And apart from a small contingent of volunteers for the Sudan War in 1885 and some 16,000 who fought in the Boer War (1899-1902), Australians took no part in even distant battles till 1914.

Exclusionists and Emancipists

With no pressures toward closing their ranks against outsiders, Australian pioneers had wide scope for falling out with each other. The historian may doubt whether there was any more quarrelsome society in the world than early New South Wales, though even at this period quarrels were usually fought out in law courts, drawing rooms, and grog shops with words and fists rather than with more lethal weapons. Naturally, indeed inevitably, the traditionally hallowed class distinctions of England tended to be reproduced in the Antipodes. In some ways conditions even accentuated them. For many years after the first settlement—up to at least 1840—the vast majority of working-class people were convicts, or ex-convicts, or people who associated familiarly with these groups and their children. Thus a visiting ship captain wrote in 1805:

> The circumstances under which the colony was settled, and the very purpose of the settlement, has had a very visible effect upon the general manners, or what may be called the national character, of Botany Bay. The free settlers are not without something of the contagion. . . . From upwards of a hundred families who have been sent out from England, there are not above eight or ten between whom and the convicts the smallest degree of discrimination could be drawn.[1]

Under these conditions it was not surprising that the colonial "gentry," at first nearly all naval or military or civilian government officers, should have drawn their spiritual skirts closely about them in an effort to fix between themselves and the "felonry" an even greater gulf than existed between the gentry and the "lower orders" in contemporary Britain. The two parties early came to be known as "exclusionists" and "emancipists," the former because they sought to exclude from polite society ex-convicts and all other low fellows, the latter because they were emancipated prisoners or friends and associates of such people. John Hood hardly exaggerated when he wrote as late as 1843: "Caste in Hindostan is not more rigidly regarded than it is in Australia: the bond and free, emancipist and exclusionist, seldom associate together familiarly."[2]

This deep and bitter class feeling was sharpened too by the fact that there were relatively few middle-class people to serve as any kind of bridge between the masses, tainted with the stigma of felonry, and those who considered themselves the colonial gentry. As late as

---

[1] John Turnbull, *A Voyage Round the World in the Years 1800, 1801, 1802, 1803, 1804,* 3 Vols. (London, 1805), Vol. 3, pp. 182-185.

[2] *Australia and the East etc.* (London, 1843) for this and following references to John Hood's views.

1841 the New South Wales census listed 4,477 squatters (large-scale graziers), merchant-importers, bankers, and professional men, and 50,158 craftsmen, laborers, servants and so on. Between these upper and lower millstones there were only 1,774 "shop-keepers and other retail dealers." In the foundation years the absence of any middle order of people was, as we have seen, even more marked. As David Collins, the colony's first judge-advocate, noted:

> It was to have been wished, that a watch . . . had been formed of free people . . . but there was not any choice. The military had their line of duty marked out for them, and between them and the convict there was no description of people from whom overseers and watchmen could be provided.[3]

Yet despite these factors, the gulf between the two classes was never as unbridgeable as those who came to be ironically termed "pure merinos" (rigid exclusionists) wished to make it. From the beginning there were other, and even more powerful, leveling influences at work. First, the very intensity of the exclusionists' emphasis on their gentility betrayed the precariousness of their position. The British class structure could not in the nature of things survive, without modification, transplantation to an antipodean wilderness—especially with its vital middle component missing. If the colonial working people were heavily tainted by convictism, so were their self-appointed betters by their position as something not very clearly distinguishable from slaveowners. As the celebrated naturalist, Charles Darwin, who visited Sydney in 1836, put it:

> How thoroughly odious to every feeling, to be waited on by a man who the day before, perhaps, was flogged from your representation, for some trifling misdemeanour. The female servants are, of course, much worse; hence children learn the vilest expressions, and it is fortunate if not equally vile ideas.[4]

Moreover, though a few of the squatters and other "pure merinos," especially after about 1820, came from families recognized in Britain as gentry, the great majority of the exclusionists did not. For the most part, members of the colonial upper class came from the middle or lower middle class in England. Often they were distinguished from the generality of colonists only by their greater wealth—and their

---

[3] *Account of the English Colony in New South Wales etc.* (London, 1798), pp. 77-79.
[4] *A Naturalist's Voyage etc.* (London: edn. 1889), p. 531.

greater taste for vulgar display. As the well-bred Hood lamented in 1843:

> If the truth must be told, the fortunes of many of the exclusionists themselves were not acquired by the purest means; close contracts, the gin or rum-shop, embarrassments wilfully created by insidious loans and ejectments, and other crooked paths, were used equally by both parties, bond and free.[2]

Or as the radical Presbyterian parson, Rev. Dr. John Dunmore Lang, put it: "*Very* strange tales are told of gentlemen of New South Wales."

Worse, from the point of view of the traditionalists, was the extreme fluidity of colonial society. Many emancipists like Simeon Lord and Samuel Terry, the "Botany Bay millionaire" who once owned the land on which Sydney's general post office now stands, rapidly became rich, and if they themselves were never quite accepted in polite society, their offspring often were. "Their children are sent to the colleges of England," wrote Hood, "and their daughters' fortunes get them husbands from among the free."

The truth was that the convict system tended to corrupt the manners, if not always the morals, of both the prisoners and their jailers. For the first thirty years or so men outnumbered women by at least four to one and most of the women, if not already hardened prostitutes when they were convicted, became such during the long voyage in the transports. Female convicts, on disembarkation, were usually "assigned" to the free settlers, as were many of the male convicts, though others were kept by "government" to carry out public works. Technically the settler acquired a property in the services of the convict, not in his or her person; but in practice officers, officials, and other free persons selected female convicts, more or less openly, as mistresses. There were of course honorable and honored exceptions, men like Governor Phillip and the much-loved Governor Lachlan Macquarie who ruled from 1810 to 1821; but Governor Philip Gidley King (1800-1806) had two sons by convict mistresses, and "Mad Tom Davey," who ruled the island dependency of Van Diemen's Land (later Tasmania) as Lieutenant-Governor from 1813 to 1817, in his official capacity attended divine service with a convict paramour on his arm. True, Davey was dismissed, but when viceroys conducted themselves thus, what was to be expected of the felonry? In fact at least up to the end of Macquarie's reign, the great majority of all the children born in the colony were illegitimate, being quaintly if prophetically termed in official documents "national children." About nine-tenths were the offspring of convicts or ex-convicts on at least one side of the (often temporary) parental union.

"The Rum Corps"

The general debauchery was both sustained and aggravated by the oceanic tide of Bengal rum which was for many years the principal commodity imported. It was an age of prodigious drinking in which the prime minister, William Pitt the Younger, despite his formidable nightly intake of port, was said to have been seen drunk in the House of Commons only once: but the specially selected colonists at Sydney and Hobart Town outdrank all others. The New South Wales Corps, recruited for the peculiar service of keeping order at "Botany Bay," replaced the Marine detachment on Phillip's departure in 1792. It proved a thorn in the flesh of successive governors from 1795 till its departure in 1810, earning in popular usage the sobriquet of "The Rum Corps." During its existence, and for a few years afterwards, coinage was in such chronically short supply that rum became the commonest medium of incentive payments to convicts and the commonest article of barter, so common that some historians have held that rum functioned as the *de facto* currency of the colony during this period. The traditional words of "The Convicts' Rum Song" give a romanticized, or heroic, picture of the place rum occupied in the community and hint at the reasons for its importance:

> Cut yer name across me backbone,
> Stretch me skin across a drum,
> Iron me up to Pinchgut Island
> From today till Kingdom-come!

> I will eat yer Norfolk dumpling
> Like a juicy Spanish plum,
> Even dance the Newgate Hornpipe
> If ye'll only gimme RUM!

"Pinchgut Island," originally little more than a barren rock in Sydney Harbor, served as a place of solitary confinement, and occasionally of execution, for particularly refractory convicts in the early days. Later officially renamed Fort Denison, its older name has persisted in popular usage. A "Norfolk dumpling" symbolizes prison conditions at Norfolk Island, on the whole the most appalling of all penal settlements for twice-convicted felons. The "Newgate hornpipe" meant, of course, the "dance" of death on the gallows. Nevertheless legend has exaggerated the quantity, though not the quality, of brutality inflicted on the "government men" under the convict system. Probably only about a tenth of all those transported ever saw the inside of such penal hells as Norfolk Island, and probably fewer than half were ever flogged at all. Soldiers in the army, equally subject to the lash, very often committed crimes in Australia because they were convinced that they would probably be better off as convicts. There were many humane and reasonable men like Darcy Wentworth among employers, as well as some sadists. Alexander Harris, one of the most judicious reporters of early Australian life, has left two accounts[5] which together show vividly the worst and the best sides of "the system." The first is an eyewitness account of a flogging, the second a convict's own tale of the brighter side of the picture:

I saw a man walk across the yard with the blood that had run from his lacerated flesh squashing out of his shoes at every step he took. A dog was licking the blood off the triangles, and the ants were carrying away great pieces of human flesh that the lash had scattered about the ground. The scourger's foot had worn a deep hole in the ground by the violence with which he whirled himself round on it to strike the quivering and wealed back, out of which stuck the sinews, white, ragged and swollen. The infliction was a hundred lashes, at about half-minute time, so as to extend the punishment through nearly an hour. . . . They had a pair of scourgers, who gave one another spell and spell about; and they were bespattered with blood like a couple of butchers. I tell you this on the authority of my own eyes. It brought my heart into my mouth.

The narrator of the following story was a convict who had absconded from the penal settlement at Coal River, later Newcastle. He was captured and brought before the bench for sentence:

Then was my turn; but old Dr. Wentworth was on the bench, and you know I had been sent to him for six weeks in harvest directly after I came into the country. . . . So, all of a sudden, just as I thought I was going to get my dowry, up jumps the old doctor, stamping as if he was mad, and shaking his fist at me. "Gentlemen," says he, "this is one of the most polished scamps in the Colony. I know him well. Two hundred lashes! Pooh, pooh! He'd forget all about it by tomorrow morning. I fancy I'd better have him down at my Homebush farm and see what I can do with him." . . . So it was agreed on, for none of the other magistrates dared say No when Darcy Wentworth said Yes. . . . So there I was by that night at sundown eating and drinking the best there was in the huts at Homebush; and you heard tell how

[5] Settlers and Convicts, ed. C. M. H. Clark (Melbourne, 1953), pp. 12-13; and The Secrets of Alexander Harris, ed. G. Carr-Harris (Sydney, 1961), pp. 107-109.

all the doctor's men live. There I stayed till I got free; and then hired to him. Never got one lash the whole five years I was with him.

The prevalence of rum, like the foundation of Australia itself, also owes something to America. When Phillip, worn out and ill, left for England no new governor had been appointed. Major Francis Grose, commandant of the New South Wales Corps, became lieutenant-governor. Soon after his assumption of power the Yankee ship *Hope* sailed through Sydney Heads with a much-needed cargo of general provisions and 7,500 gallons of rum. Her skipper, Benjamin Page, declared that he would not sell his mixed cargo unless every barrel of rum was also purchased. Supplies of all kinds were still desperately short and Page, like other trading skippers, demanded absurdly inflated prices for his goods. In the face of such extortionate demands, the officers of the Corps and their friends decided to form a counter-monopoly of their own. Under the nominal command of Grose, but largely inspired by a forceful young lieutenant called John Macarthur, they combined to purchase, without competition, the whole cargo of the *Hope*—and of most other ships which came to the colony for years afterwards. Soon the soldiers of the Corps found that their wages were being paid partly or wholly in rum or other trade goods, all of which were valued by the officers' junta at absurdly high rates. In this way poor settlers, mostly emancipated or time-expired convicts, and even those still serving their sentences, were also exploited by the exclusionist monopolists; for it had early been discovered that as an incentive to efficient work, the scourger's cat-o'-nine-tails, no matter how furiously and continually plied, was insufficient. The convicts, therefore, were allowed to seek private employment in the late afternoons after their "government work" for the day had been done. When Phillip left the officers of the Corps lost little time in extending this privilege, especially by withdrawing many more convicts altogether from government work and assigning them to themselves and their friends. The number of lashes inflicted hardly decreased but the amount of rum in circulation increased mightily.

Three more naval governors, John Hunter, Philip King, and William Bligh, tried unavailingly to break the rum traffic and to mitigate the social and economic evils which it nourished. Instead their own careers were blighted by the entrenched influence of the monopolists. Bligh, who governed from 1806 till 1808, was actually deposed in a local *coup d'etat* carried out by the "Rum Corps"—the very body whose prime function it was to uphold his authority. A few days before Phillip's First Fleet sailed from England in May 1787, Bligh's crew had mutinied in H. M. S. *Bounty* near Tahiti. The story is well known and has caused posterity to think of Bligh as a blustering and brutal bully. True, but the record shows he was a good deal more than that. How else could he have brought safely to Timor, a distance of 3,600 miles, the open boat in which he was set adrift, overloaded as it was with eighteen men and boys who refused to join the mutineers? As governor of New South Wales, Bligh's determined efforts to curb the power of the rum traders rapidly made him very popular with the "little men" of the community, particularly with the struggling emancipist farmers of the Hawkesbury River district some twenty-five miles north-west of Sydney. They made him equally unpopular with the officers of the Corps and the exclusionists.

Of these the most influential was John Macarthur (1767-1834), who came of an old Jacobite family and who had the ear of powerful friends in England. With his wife and infant son he arrived in 1791 as a lieutenant of the New South Wales Corps. Though he never became a senior officer, the strength of his character was such that, almost from the beginning, he dominated the exclusionist faction and, more narrowly, the junta of military and civilian officers which led the rum monopoly. Yet he enriched Australia as well as himself by his sheep-breeding experiments, and is rightly remembered as the principal founder of the country's great wool industry. Gentle and virtuous in his family life, his overweening pride drove him to quarrel violently with any man who crossed his designs. One of his many enemies called him "as sharp as a razor and as rapacious as a shark," and Governors Hunter, King, and Bligh denounced him in scarcely less baleful terms as, among other things, "the grand perturbator." Toward the end of his life his turbulent passions ended in madness. At the time of the "Rum Rebellion" he had been thrown into jail by the courts, formally for a minor breach of the law but in fact more for his obstinate and successful defense of the monopolists' interests. From prison he engineered the junta's bloodless coup, which was actually carried out by Major George Johnston, commander of the Corps and lieutenant-governor of the colony. On the twentieth anniversary of the first landing, 26 January 1808, with band playing and colors flying, the "Rum Corps" carried out what some cynics have termed its only martial action. The soldiers marched on Government House and arrested Bligh. A contemporary print shows him being dragged from his hiding place under a bed; but in view of his naval record it seems likely that this was a piece of rebel propaganda. Johnston and the junta took over the government, continued to import rum, and proceeded to grant more land to themselves and their friends. After some years Johnston was cashiered by a London court-martial. Macarthur was not allowed to return to Australia for some

time, but his wife Elizabeth capably looked after his colonial interests
during his absence.

Progress Under Macquarie

The "Rum Rebellion" at least prompted His Majesty's ministers to
give an unwonted modicum of thought to affairs in New South Wales.
The system by which naval governors had to depend for their authority on the good will of a military force, which distance made semi-
autonomous in practice, was abandoned. On New Year's Day 1810
Lieutenant-Colonel Lechlan Macquarie, at the head of his own regiment of 73rd Highlanders, assumed office as governor. For the next
eleven years he ruled New South Wales and its dependencies in
much the same absolute but paternalistic spirit as some of his ancestors had ruled their Highland clans. During his regime (1810-1821)
the power of the rum monopolists was broken, not so much because
of the loyalty of his regiment or even his own prodigious efforts, as
because the rising native-born generation, an increasing trickle of free
immigrants, and growing export trade in whale oil and sealskins
rendered a nearly closed monopolistic system no longer economically
viable. He closed scores of licensed taverns while sly-grog shops
multiplied, for if the monopoly of rum was ended, the rate of its
consumption hardly lessened. He gave to the central Sydney area
the basic street plan it has today. He ordered the erection of many
fine buildings. Among those still standing are St. James' Church in
King Street, the adjoining Hyde Park convict barracks, St. Matthew's
Church at Windsor and the graceful Georgian building for long
known as the "Rum Hospital." Only part of the last still stands and
serves as the Parliament House of the state of New South Wales. Its
name derived from the fact that, in his efforts to stamp out the rum
trade, Macquarie at one stage thought to control it by granting to
three contractors (not including Macarthur!) an *official* three years'
monopoly of the import of spirits. In return they built the hospital.
History will never know how much more rum was smuggled into
the colony or illicitly distilled there.

Macquarie's chief architect was an emancipist who had been transported for forgery, Francis Greenway, whom future generations have
agreed to honor as an artist in brick and stone. The new governor
consistently encouraged merit wherever he found it, even inviting
deserving emancipists to dine at his table. In his view, as perhaps it
will prove in the long-term view of history, the emancipists, with all
their sins upon their heads, had done more for the prosperity and
good order of the colony than had their exclusionist betters. During
the last two years of his term the British Government sent out an

able lawyer, J. T. Bigge, to report on the colony and on Macquarie's administration of it. The Old Viceroy's view of the factions in New South Wales was made clear in a letter he wrote to Commissioner Bigge during 1819. Here is an extract with emphatically muddled syntax and indignantly explosive capitals, just as it sputtered from his quill:

You already know that Nine-tenths of the population of this Colony are or have been Convicts, or the Children of Convicts. You have Yet perhaps to learn that these are the people who have Quietly submitted to the Laws and Regulations of the Colony, altho' informed by the *Free Settlers* and some of the Officers of Government that they were illegal: these are the Men who have tilled the Ground, who have built Houses and Ships, who have made wonderful Efforts, Considering the Disadvantages under which they have Acted, in Agriculture, in Maritime Speculations, and in Manufactures; these are the Men who, placed in the balance as Character, both Moral and political (at least since their Arrival here) in the opposite Scale to those Free Settlers (who Struggle for their Depression) whom you will find to preponderate.

We have seen that bitter class feelings existed in Australia before Macquarie's time. Perhaps his emancipist policy did something to accentuate them. It certainly did in the opinion of leading exclusionist spokesmen like Macarthur, who successfully obtained the ear of Bigge and decisively influenced the tenor of his official report. More than ever the emancipists and their children felt that Australia, as it was beginning to be called, was *their* country, founded for them and their descendants. Yet Macquarie's period had also instituted profound changes that were to strengthen even more in the long run the influence of the free immigrants.

When he sailed for Britain, New South Wales was no longer primarily a prison farm measuring some forty miles from east to west and from north to south, extensive by British standards, it is true, but still hemmed in between the Blue Mountains and the Pacific. In 1813 a way across the range had been found by a party which included young W. C. Wentworth, son of the old doctor, and one of the first and most illustrious native-born Australians. Six years later he wrote of the western plains stretching away beyond the Great Divide that they were "admirably suited for the pasture of sheep, the wool of which will without doubt eventually become the principal export of this colony, and may be conveyed across the mountains at an inconsiderable expense." Not everyone at the time shared Wentworth's vision. Nevertheless almost limitless pastures for the expansion of the wool industry stood waiting. The Bank of New South

Wales, first in importance today after the government-owned Commonwealth Bank, was founded in 1817 mainly by some successful emancipists with the governor's encouragement. Cedar cutting in the coastal brushes had joined whaling and sealing to furnish profitable export commodities. Wholesale importers and traders were firmly established in Sydney and Hobart, and retail trading had begun. Few people still depended directly on the communal government store, as all had done in the foundation years and most still did on Macquarie's arrival. Bigge's *Report* to the home government urged that extensive parcels of land, principally for stock raising, should be granted to respectable free immigrants in proportion to the amount of capital they brought with them to invest. With cheap assigned convict labor, the profits to be made in pastoralism were very tempting, and an increasing stream of well-to-do free immigrants arrived to take advantage of the new arrangements. But the harvest lay for the most part in the future. Only the seeds had been planted during Macquarie's regime, some of them unwittingly. In any case, the old chieftain received little official credit for his exertions. Bigge's *Report* condemned his emancipist policy and his "extravagant" building program—unjustly as it has seemed to posterity. At the same time, the report recognized economic reality by advocating the development of a large-scale wool industry for the future, thereby at least tacitly condemning the efforts of past governors to carry out government policy; for, insofar as the Home authorities can be said to have had a positive economic policy for the colony, it had been to encourage the development of a large class of (mainly emancipist) small-holding agriculturists. Macquarie was given an affectionate farewell by thousands of his subjects. When he sailed for the last time out of Sydney Harbor in the *Surry* on 15 February 1822, New South Wales was considerably more prosperous, and somewhat less turbulent and wicked, than it had been on his arrival.

Currency Reform

Much has been written in this chapter of the depravity of early Australian society. It would be misleading to end it without mentioning moral changes for the better which were already becoming visible before Macquarie's departure. In 1811 T. W. Plummer wrote that officers, private soldiers, settlers, and other free inhabitants all chose female assignees "not only as servants but as avowed objects of intercourse, which is without even the plea of the slightest previous attachment as an excuse, rendering the whole colony little less than an extensive brothel." [6] Other evidence shows that, though this may have been a polemical statement, it was hardly an exaggerated one. Governor Hunter wrote in 1798:

> A more wicked, abandoned, and irreligious set of people have never been brought together in any part of the world . . . order and morality is not the wish of the inhabitants; it interferes with the private views and pursuits of individuals of various descriptions.

The "national children" of the official documents were known popularly as "currency lads and lasses," originally because, like the makeshift local currency of the early days—Spanish dollars with "dumps" punched out of their centers, traders' tokens, notes-of-hand, and so forth—they were a local product not imported from Britain as were free immigrants, convicts, and a trickle of sterling coinage. Many of these currency children could hardly have known who their parents were. Perhaps they were better off than those who did, since most of their fathers were drunken and demoralized habitual criminals, and most of their mothers equally drunken and demoralized prostitutes. Small wonder that contemporaries feared the worst for the thousands of "national children" growing up in these conditions. For the first twenty-five years or so of Australia's history observers were almost unanimous in expecting that the native-born would reproduce the manners and morals of their progenitors. Yet no such thing happened.

Commissioner Bigge, we have seen, was by no means predisposed to view the convict and emancipist classes favorably. Yet in his *Report on Agriculture and Trade*, issued in 1823, occurs the classic statement on the transformation of their children:

> The class of inhabitants that have been born in the colony affords a remarkable exception to the moral and physical character of their parents: they are generally tall in person, and slender in their limbs, of fair complexion and small features. They are capable of undergoing more fatigue, and are less exhausted by labour than native Europeans; they are active in their habits but remarkably awkward in their movements. In their tempers they are quick and irascible, but not vindictive; and I only repeat the testimony of persons who have had many opportunities of observing them, that they neither inherit the vices nor feelings of their parents.

[6] For source of this and following passages on "Currency Reform" see Ken Macnab and Russel Ward, "Nature and Nurture of the First Generation of Native-Born Australians," in *Historical Studies: Australia and New Zealand* (Melbourne), November 1962.

There is not the slightest doubt that such a reform did take place. Contemporary evidence is practically unanimous. For instance Peter Cunningham, a hard-headed Scots surgeon, wrote in 1827 of "the open and manly simplicity of character displayed by this part of our population . . . [which] . . . was little tainted by the vices so prominent among their parents. . . . Drunkenness is almost unknown to them, and honesty proverbial." And in 1834 even the dour Reverend Lang, whose talent for nosing out human wickedness was possibly unrivaled in the whole continent, wrote:

> I am happy, indeed, to be able to state, as the result of ten years' extensive observation in the colony, that drunkenness is by no means a vice to which the colonial youth of either sex are at all addicted. Reared in the very midst of scenes of drunkenness of the most revolting description and of daily occurrence, they are almost uniformly temperate; for if there are exceptions, as I do acknowledge there are a few, the wonder, I had almost said the miracle, is that they have not been tenfold more numerous.

The most convincing evidence is probably that of Sir William Burton, a Justice of the New South Wales Supreme Court from 1833 until 1844. He was so impressed by the law-abiding nature of the currency people that he inquired closely into the criminal statistics of the time. From his data it has been shown that the first generation of native-born Australians were, at least in a statistical legal sense, *more* virtuous than any other class in the community including that of the free immigrants. Over the five-year period 1833-1837, for instance, the average number of persons tried annually before Burton, per thousand of each of the four classes of people in the colony, was as follows: *Convict*, 3.4; *Emancipist*, 3.2; *Free Immigrant*, 1.3; *Currency*, 1.0 Further, none of the crimes committed by currency people in this period, Burton maintained, were of an atrocious kind punishable by death; and nearly half (thirteen out of thirty) were for stock-stealing, generally known as "cattle-duffing"—an activity not held to be criminal at all by popular Australian opinion until almost the present century. Robert D. Barton, uncle of "Banjo" Paterson and a respectable squatter, as an old man in 1917 could still write, without conscious humor:

> The young Australians were, I think, strictly honest as regards money or valuables; you could leave your hut or house with everything open for days, perhaps weeks, and when you returned you would miss nothing, except, perhaps, that someone had made a pot of tea or got a feed, which, of course, they were all entitled to, and never refused. But, from my earliest recollections, the branding of other people's calves

was not looked upon as a crime, . . . and the killing of cattle for meat on the place was almost invariably done at someone else's expense. However, that condition of things gradually changed, but a great many men never realised the change . . . but continued their depredations, which were then called cattle-stealing.

How did these currency men and women rise above the influence of their parents? Not by a miracle, as the Rev. Lang was tempted to suppose. The main reason was simply that, compared with those in Great Britain at the time, Australian conditions offered a very good living to anyone able and willing to work. There was an almost continuous labor shortage, especially in the bush; partly because in a seemingly limitless wilderness inhabited by very few people the sheer quantity of urgently necessary work also seemed to be limitless, and partly because so much of the labor force was highly inefficient. We have already seen how convicts had to be bribed with incentive payments to improve upon the "government-stroke" which was their preferred, go-slow method of working. Yet most employers found convict labor much more efficient than that of most free immigrants, who were unaccustomed to Australian conditions. Under these conditions free *and* experienced labor was at such a premium that even children could command good wages—and did. It seems incredible, but contemporary documents abound with evidence of boys ten to fifteen years old carrying out responsible and sometimes lonely jobs. Thirteen- and fourteen-year-olds commonly drove bullock-teams on long cross-country journeys or, like young Albert Wright, for many years managed a remote western sheep-station, alone except for one half-mad shepherd. Thus, colonial conditions provided the economic opportunity for young people to become precociously self-reliant. At the same time, vicious home conditions made most of those currency children who *had* homes only too anxious to run away from them. The environment was such as to enable and promote the reaction of currency children away from overtly depraved convict-emancipist characteristics. Thus Bigge's *Report on the State of the Colony* (1822) noted that young currency men were unwilling to marry convict women, owing "chiefly to a sense of pride in the native-born youths, approaching to contempt for the vices and depravity of the convicts even when manifested in the persons of their own parents."

There were of course other convict-emancipist attitudes, not necessarily vicious in themselves—such as group loyalty, or hatred of informers and of affected manners—which the rising generation of young Australians saw no reason to reject. Historians have too long been mesmerized by the horrors of the convict system and the depravity of its victims, forgetting the Gospel statement that a man is never defiled by what is done to him, but only by his own deeds. In this perspective early Australian history surely gives much cause for pride and none for shame. From the most unpromising possible material there developed in a few short years the self-reliant progenitors of a free and generous people. By 1821 New South Wales had begun to be something much more than the miserable slave farm which had been founded thirty-three years earlier. Not only was a vigorous and self-respecting generation of native-born people growing up, but a new class of respectable free immigrants, not mainly dependent upon the colonial civil or military establishments, had begun to make its appearance.

THREE

New Pastures and New Attitudes

1821-1851

Between 1821 and 1851 important new colonies were founded on remote parts of the Australian coastline, much of the habitable interior was effectively occupied by pastoralists and their men, and a distinctively Australian ethos began to take shape, at least among the mass of the population if not so much among the more cultivated minority. At the same time the colonies were moving steadily toward self-government. We shall consider these major developments and some of the relationships between them—political reform, the planting of new settlements, the great "squatting rush" to the interior, and the growth of a characteristic outlook. All of these developments were strongly influenced in one way or another by the convict system, for the importation of felons to mainland eastern Australia continued until 1840, and to Van Diemen's Land until 1852—after which the island colony was known as Tasmania. In fact, the great majority of all convicts sent to Australia were transported during these years.

Growth of Representative Government

Macquarie is sometimes called "the last of the tyrants" because representative institutions increasingly limited the governors' powers during the thirty years or so following his retirement. In accordance with Bigge's *Report,* an act of the British Parliament in 1823 instituted certain legal reforms in Australia, separated the administration of Van Diemen's Land from that of New South Wales, and gave the latter colony a Legislative Council. True, the Council consisted of only a few officials nominated by the governor himself, and he could ignore their advice if he thought it wise to do so; but the chief justice now had to certify that every new ordinance was "consistent with the laws of England, so far as the circumstances of the colony will permit." That the governor's powers were no longer absolute was shown in 1827 when a liberal-minded chief justice of New South Wales, Sir Francis Forbes, refused to certify a law which sought to censor the colonial press. Partly as a result of this squabble, another imperial act of 1828 increased the size of the Council to fifteen. The power of veto was transferred from the chief justice to the Supreme Court, but all the Council members were still nominated by the governor. Eight of them were to be his chief administrative officials and seven were "unofficial" members, usually in practice leading exclusionists. Since the governor alone could introduce legislation, it is not surprising that disagreements between him and the Council were at first unusual.

This remained the constitutional position until 1842, but throughout the period agitation for a greater measure of self-government increased. Most prominent in the movement was William Charles Wentworth (1790-1872) who, as a young currency lad, had helped to find a way across the mountain barrier. His father, D'Arcy Wentworth, a connection of Earl Fitzwilliam, after being acquitted at the Old Bailey of highway robbery, had volunteered to join the second fleet as a surgeon. In New South Wales bond and free workmen thought him one of the best masters "that ever lived in the world." Young William Charles was educated at Cambridge University where he was runner-up for the Chancellor's Medal for poetry in 1823, but his mother had been a convict girl. By the 1840's he had become the most famous living Australian, yet such was the exaggerated *hauteur* of the exclusionists that as late as 1863 T. S. Mort, a successful Sydney businessman of middle-class but "untainted" background, could speak thus, without intentional humor, of Wentworth:

> I have never met him in society as he did not move in the same spheres as myself. Had he visited with the principal families in the colony at the time I must have met him, as I exchanged visits with nearly the whole of them.[1]

Thus, as long as the convict system lasted, the bitter faction strife between emancipists and exclusionists helped to defer the granting of more liberal political institutions. Having already started a newspaper, *The Australian*, Wentworth in 1835 took a leading part in founding the Australian Patriotic Association. Composed mainly of emancipists and their sympathizers, this body yet established an influential lobby in the House of Commons and agitated for a representative legislature and other liberal institutions. Led by James Macarthur, son of the grand perturbator, the exclusionists lobbied Parliament even more effectively. If reform was inevitable they wished to limit it, seeking at most extension of the powers of a larger, but

[1] Alan Barrard, *Visions and Profits* (Melbourne, 1961), p. 20.

still nominated, Council. Both factions desired the continuation of
the convict system which provided the cheap labor on which their
wealth depended; yet the British Government remained obstinately
of the opinion that free institutions should not be granted to a society
whose population still comprised a majority of convicted or emancipated felons and their descendants. Some of the latter who, with a
few immigrant artisans made up the embryonic working class of
Sydney, had not much influence on events. When the Patriotic
Association declared for the continuance of transportation in 1838,
most working men withdrew their support. At the same time, the
wealthy emancipists and the exclusionists began to find more common
ground in politics, if not yet in social life.

The impasse was resolved in London rather than Sydney. In 1837-
38 a select committee of the House of Commons, under the chair-
manship of Sir William Molesworth, heard voluminous evidence and
recommended the abolition of transportation to New South Wales.
Practically no more convicts were sent to eastern mainland Australia
after 1840, and in 1842 the membership of the Legislative Council
was increased to thirty-six, two-thirds of whom were to be elected.
Moreover elected members might introduce topics for debate. However, the franchise was fixed so that only a minority of citizens could
vote, and no one could be elected to the Council unless he owned
property worth at least £2,000—equivalent to something like $70,000
in terms of today's money values. The governor retained the power
of nominating the twelve official members who remained responsible
to him, and he retained control of Crown lands and the right, in the
last resort, to veto any measure. Thus the new Council was not a
very democratic body. Because of its composition it was often far
more conservative in outlook than the Queen's representative himself. It was sometimes termed "the Squatters' Council" because
wealthy pastoralists tended to dominate its deliberations and spent a
disproportionate amount of time wrangling with Governor Sir George
Gipps (1838-1846) over the conditions under which Crown lands
were to be leased to themselves and their friends. Nevertheless, the
"Squatters' Council" did provide valuable training in the art of self-
government. It acted, to some extent, as a genuine sounding board
for public opinion. Its debates were fully reported in the newspapers
and discussed, sometimes with passionate interest, by the colonists.

Since convicts could no longer be sent to the mainland, many more,
relatively, were shipped to Van Diemen's Land during the 1840's.
For a period at the beginning of this decade New South Wales
suffered from a severe labor shortage at the very time when insufficient
work could be found for the mass of convict and emancipist labor in

Van Diemen's Land. The island dependency, since convictism continued, had to remain discontented with its nominated Legislative Council.

Western Australia

In 1840 the territory of New South Wales still included most of eastern Australia, roughly the areas of present-day Queensland, Victoria, and the eastern part of the Northern Territory, in addition to that which still constitutes the mother colony; but by that date all the other major colonies had been founded in fact if not in legal form. Oddly enough, Britain never laid formal claim to the western third of New Holland until nearly forty years after the first settlement at Sydney. Possibly there was a vague feeling that it belonged to the Dutch who, however, continued to show no interest in it. In 1826 the British Government, fearing supposed French designs, claimed Western Australia. A small party of forty-four soldiers and convicts under Major Lockyer raised the Union Jack at King George's Sound on Christmas Day 1826. Albany, as the King George's Sound settlement came to be called, was about 1,800 miles distant by sea from the nearest white settlement at Hobart. It was even further by land from the east coast settlements near Sydney: but until 1917, when the transcontinental railway was built, there was no land communication between western Australia and the rest of the country. Waterless deserts between barred the way to all but a handful of hardy explorers and their camels. Western Australia's extreme physical isolation is perhaps the main reason why it was developed so much later than all the other colonies. Another was the generally sandy, barren nature of the coastal plain on which the main settlement at Perth was founded three years after the first outpost at King George's Sound. A third handicap was the absence of a "convict establishment"—and of the cheap labor and government investment of capital which convictism brought with it.

In the 1820's the growth of the wool industry in New South Wales was beginning to attract the attention of private British investors. A group of capitalists of whom the most important was Thomas Peel, a second cousin of the statesman Sir Robert Peel, thought that money might be made in Western Australia. The government was persuaded that the scheme might absorb some of the unemployed in Britain. It agreed to grant capitalists land at the Swan River settlement, at the rate of forty acres for every £3 invested, if they would pay the passages of free laborers. No convicts were to be sent. In return for a promise to land 400 settlers Thomas Peel was granted 250,000 acres. He selected land most of which is still worth little today. The government's only role was to pay the civil and military officers. Captain James Stirling, the first governor, landed and proclaimed the new colony on 18 June 1829.

The Swan River settlement long remained a sickly infant. Because the land was almost given away, the few laborers who came to the new colony generally chose to scratch a subsistence from their own blocks rather than to work for increasingly impoverished employers. Most of the latter had no experience of conditions in Australia, and they were too far away from the older settlements to learn very much from earlier colonists. Some of the most able and enterprising immigrants, like the Henty brothers, who pioneered sheep-raising in what was to become Victoria a few years later, moved on to the more prosperous eastern colonies. Under Edward Gibbon Wakefield's influence land became progressively more expensive after 1831, but the shortage of labor and capital persisted. In the whole of Western Australia, an area of about 1,000,000 square miles which is mostly desert, there were only 2,760 white people in 1841 (twelve years after the first landing), and in 1851 there were only 7,186. By that time, however, the colonists themselves had petitioned the Home government to send them convicts. The first shipload reached Fremantle in June 1850, and Western Australia received 10,000 male convicts between that date and 1868, when transportation was finally abandoned. The labor of these men helped to set the colony on its feet, but development continued to be relatively sluggish until the Western Australian gold rush of the 1890's brought a sudden influx of immigrants from the eastern colonies.

South Australia

The story of South Australia is inseparably linked with the name of Wakefield, leading spirit among the reforming "theoretical colonizers" who considerably influenced British colonial policy at this time. A brilliant, ambitious, but unstable character, in 1816 he married under rather shady circumstances a beautiful young heiress. After her death he tricked into marriage another rich minor but was sentenced this time to three years in London's Newgate Gaol where, appropriately enough, he wrote his *Letters from Sydney*. These newspaper articles, published as a book entitled *A Letter from Sydney and Other Writings* in 1829, set forth his leading ideas on "systematic colonization." The blessings of British civilization must be transferred *in toto* to overseas settlements. To achieve this, land must be sold at a "sufficient price" to ensure that laborers and mechanics could not too readily acquire land of their own. Thus, he argued, due subordination of men to their masters and a proper, or British, relationship between the classes would be maintained. At the same time, the "sufficient price" would prevent that dispersion of settlement which was tending so much to the encouragement of lawlessness in New South Wales, for no man would buy dear land situated far away from towns and markets. Finally, the proceeds of land sales should be used to bring out laborers so that the process should be self-sustaining. Wakefield was too shrewd ever to translate his "sufficient price" into a cash equivalent, and he died holding that his theory had never been given a fair trial in South Australia or later in New Zealand. Nevertheless, his ideas had some effect on policy. The minimum price of Crown lands in New South Wales was raised to five shillings an acre in 1831, to twelve shillings in 1838, and in 1842 to £1 an acre in all the Australian colonies. The extent of Wakefield's influence on South Australia is suggested by the fact that, from the landing of the first settlers there in 1836, the minimum price of land was £1.

In the founding of South Australia there was a greater measure of idealism than in that of the other Australian colonies. It was not a colony but a "province," and transportation of convicts was to play no part in its history—facts which many South Australians are still quick to mention today. Radical politicians, systematic colonizers, non-Conformist bankers, and "reforming" speculators all played a part in its establishment, and some of them settled there. Among the immigrants there were relatively fewer penniless, unskilled laborers and many fewer Irish people, than among those who shipped to the other colonies. There were relatively many more artisans and other respectable, industrious middle-class people, radical or liberal in politics and piously non-Conformist or evangelical Anglican in religion. As with the New England puritans, the passage of time has served only to confirm some of these traits while changing others. Adelaide is still praised by many of its own citizens as "the City of Churches," and still occasionally referred to ironically by non-South Australians as "the Holy City." Within a hundred miles of the capital are produced most of the grapes in Australia and some of the best wine in the world; yet South Australian hotels still cease serving liquor at six P.M. sharp, and even in daylight hours women may have nothing to do with the sinful business. Strong waters are sold by men usually dressed like undertakers in black alpaca coats. South Australians still tend to be almost as serious-minded as their forebears, but the material success that has often rewarded virtue has made them increasingly staid and conservative in politics. In South Australia's first decade of responsible government (1856-1866), the premiership of the province changed hands thirteen times. For the last twenty-seven years (in 1965) there has been no deviation at all from Sir Thomas Playford's Liberal–Country Party government.

The relative stability of South Australian life probably owes as much to accidents of geography as to the character of her immigrants. Adelaide was built on the southern end of a coastal plain some 150 miles long and up to about 50 miles wide. Soil and climate were ideally suited to growing wheat as well as vines, olives, and other Mediterranean-type crops. Moreover, Spencer's and St. Vincent's Gulfs penetrate this area so deeply that they provided cheap sea transport almost from the farmers' boundary fences. Beyond this small area between the Flinders Ranges and the Gulfs, most of the remainder of South Australia is very like the outback parts of New South Wales or Western Australia—semidesert or desert country which can support only a sparse and precarious existence for pastoralists. Conditions in this area were far more favorable than in any other part of Australia to the successful application of Wakefield's ideas. The sage of Newgate denounced the plan, declaring that the £1 per acre was not a "sufficient price." Nevertheless, after initial setbacks caused by delays in the land survey, by speculation, and by a division of control between the governor and the commissioners representing the founding investors and theorizers, the new province prospered steadily if unspectacularly. Unlike the Swan River settlement, it was near enough to the eastern colonies to profit by trading and other contacts with them. "Overlanders" drove thousands of head of stock to the new Adelaide market, and with them came hundreds of "old hands," as experienced ex-convict bushmen were called at the time. Their arrival was deplored by those who wished to keep the province free from the convict "taint," but with their pioneering skills the old hands could command higher wages than the free immigrant laborers could earn, and so most of them stayed on to merge with the general mass of the new colonists. By 1851, when the discovery of gold in New South Wales and Victoria brought hundreds of thousands of new immigrants there, South Australia was firmly established as the granary of the whole continent. The relatively sober and industrious character of her citizens may still strike even a casual overseas visitor. To a greater degree than is common elsewhere in Australia, South Australians came to work, to build, and to live; they did not come because they had to, or to make a quick pound before moving on. Even their barns and farm outhouses are commonly made of stone or brick, while in other states a great many houses are built of wood.

Victoria

Western Australia and South Australia were conceived, to use a horse-breeding metaphor, out of the British Government by English capitalists and theorizers. The latter colony, as we have seen, would not have prospered as it did without the unforeseen, unofficial, and in some respects illegal help of the overlanders. The Port Phillip district of New South Wales or "Australia Felix," as Victoria was variously known until 1850, was founded entirely without official sanction by these trespassers upon Crown lands. To understand we shall have to retrace our steps a little.

By the 1830's, W. C. Wentworth's vision of a great wool-growing industry on the transmontane plains of New South Wales was being realized. Pastoralists were streaming west and south and north to the unsettled, and largely unexplored, districts to grow more wool for the seemingly insatiable demands of the Yorkshire textile industry. Governor Sir Ralph Darling (1825-1831), a conscientious and formal-minded soldier, felt that his subjects were straying beyond the reach of government. In addition, he was much troubled by hundreds of convict "bolters"—absconders many of whom had become bush-rangers (highwaymen). To remedy these evils Darling in 1829 drew a roughly semicircular line on the map at a distance of about 250 miles from Sydney. This boundary line, the government declared, marked the "limits of location" beyond which no man might graze his flocks and herds. Even the most respectable colonists, alas, were unimpressed. A few years later it was said that half the sheep in New South Wales were feeding illegally beyond the boundary line. Ten years later Gipps, still plagued by the problem of governing squatters, declared:

> As well might it be attempted to confine the Arabs of the Desert within a circle traced, upon their sands, as to confine the Graziers or Woolgrowers of New South Wales within any bounds that can possibly be assigned to them.

Meanwhile, the liberal-minded Governor Sir Richard Bourke (1831-1838) had attempted to compromise with reality. In 1836 he had his Legislative Council enact regulations which recognized a squatter's right to temporary occupancy of as much Crown land as he pleased beyond the "boundaries of location," provided he paid £10 annually for a "squatting licence."

While the best grazing land within three or four hundred miles of Sydney was being taken up in this distressingly unsystematic way, Van Diemen's Land pastoralists were becoming cramped for room in the island colony, much of which was in any case mountainous, heavily forested, and unsuitable for pasture. Among them were the Henty brothers, who had tried their luck briefly in the new Swan River settlement before moving on to Van Diemen's Land. In November 1834 Edward Henty, with laborers and stock, crossed Bass Strait and squatted at Portland Bay in the then almost completely unexplored Port Phillip district. He was followed a few months later by two other parties of Vandiemonians led by John Batman and John Pascoe Fawkner, who settled in Port Phillip Bay itself on the site of the present city of Melbourne. There they were astonished to find living with the aborigines a "wild white man." His name was William Buckley, and he had absconded from a party of convicts which for three months in 1803, under the command of David Collins, had made an abortive attempt to settle at Port Phillip. Most living Australians have never heard of William Buckley, but they still speak of a man's having "Buckley's chance," or merely of his "having Buckley's," when they mean that the odds against him are so heavy as to leave him practically no chance at all.

Meanwhile officialdom was catching up with events. In 1836 the surveyor-general of New South Wales, Sir Thomas Mitchell, led an exploring party west along the Lachlan River to the Murray and then struck south through unknown country to the coast, where he found the Hentys' station already established. He named the rich grazing country he had discovered "Australia Felix," and his reports accelerated the rate at which squatters crossed from Van Diemen's Land to the new settlement, while others overlanded their flocks south from New South Wales proper. Though Governor Bourke in distant Sydney warned these unlicensed trespassers on the lands of the Crown, he knew the movement could not be stopped. By the end of the year he had secured London's authorization of the settlement as a district of New South Wales and had dispatched to it some government officials, soldiers, and convict servants. Australia Felix proved as rich a pastoral district as the firstfooters had thought. Soon free immigrants began arriving direct from Britain. Many were hardy Lowland Scots farmers and some brought capital as well as brawn and brains to invest in the new settlement. Those whose sobriety and perseverance were proof against colonial habits profited mightily. By 1850 the human and stock population of the Port Phillip district considerably surpassed that of South Australia.

In the same year the Imperial Parliament passed the Australian Colonies Government Act, which set up the Port Phillip district as the new and separate colony of Victoria. The act also gave to Victoria, Van Diemen's Land, and South Australia their own Legislative

Councils on the New South Wales model and invited all the colonies, except Western Australia where convictism was beginning instead of ending, to submit to London their own proposals for constitutional amendment.

Queensland

Meanwhile squatters had also moved into the northern part of New South Wales, later to become Queensland. In 1824 a new penal settlement had been established at the mouth of the Brisbane River in Moreton Bay. Remoteness, it was hoped, would give added security to this prison for doubly convicted felons. But by 1840 the first squatters had overlanded their flocks to the rich Darling Downs district on the western slopes of the Great Dividing Range inland from Moreton Bay. Two years later officials in Sydney again bowed to the inevitable and declared the northern district open for settlement. As the northerners grew in number they agitated, like the inhabitants of the Port Phillip District before them, for separation from New South Wales. Following the example of the Port Phillipians, they chose John Dunmore Lang to represent them in the Sydney legislature. Presbyterian divine, self-righteous moralist, radical politician, newspaper publisher, pamphleteer, and republican, Lang was surely one of the most energetic Australians of the last century. Though he probably did more than any other single man to secure separation and self-government for both Victoria and Queensland, his pugnacity made him so many powerful enemies that his name is not widely known today. The new colony of Queensland was proclaimed in 1859. Before thirty years had passed many observers were agreed that it was certainly the "most Australian," or most nationalistic, of all the colonies. To discover why, we shall have to examine more closely the nature of the great squatting rush which was largely responsible for the creation of the two new colonies to the north and south of the mother colony.

Effects of the "Squatting Rush"

This movement first gathered momentum in the 1830's. By the 1880's few areas capable of supporting one sheep to every ten acres or so remained unoccupied, though the occupation was and still is extremely sparse. Even today, over much of this area a man's nearest neighbor may live twenty or thirty miles away. The American historian Frederick Jackson Turner's "frontier thesis" is apposite to our understanding of this process. Though his theories have been subjected to searching criticism, the soundness of his basic idea is certainly borne out by Australian history. Adaptation to a strange environment naturally proceeds farthest and fastest on the advancing frontier of settlement, where conditions are most unlike those in

Europe whence the settlers or their forefathers came. In the middle of the last century new attitudes to life, new skills, and new manners were acquired far more rapidly by prairie buffalo-skinners, or by stockmen on the dry inland plains of Australia, than they were by relatively newly arrived immigrants in the eastern coastal cities of both continents. The frontiersmen's very lives often depended quite directly upon their capacity for rapid adaptation. As Turner wrote in a famous passage, "the wilderness masters the colonist." On any frontier of settlement, civilized refinements and specialist services of all kinds tend to be scarce. It is far more important to do than to speculate, to make do than to bemoan the absence of proper facilities. Thus in both countries the frontiersman tended to acquire rough-and-ready manners along with a wide range of practical skills. He became in most ways more self-reliant, more "independent," and more "democratic" than he or his ancestors had been in Europe. At the same time, his life taught him to undervalue, if not actually to scorn, intellectual, spiritual, and artistic pursuits. All this does not mean, however, that we should expect frontier conditions to evoke completely identical reactions in the two continents. After all, the two "wildernesses" differed in important ways and so tended to generate different responses.

Turner thought that the two most important effects of the frontier in the United States were to promote national unity and nationalism and to promote democracy. There is abundant evidence that in Australia too frontier conditions fostered nationalist sentiment.[2] In both countries in the last century the proportion of native-born citizens was markedly greater in the "outback" than it was in the urban areas near the coast, and these frontiersmen, mingling together in the wilderness, naturally tended to find that the accident of having been born in different colonies was no longer as important as it had seemed before they left Boston, New York, or Baltimore; Melbourne, Sydney, or Adelaide. It is true too that American and Australian frontiersmen both liked to believe that they were the most democratic people on earth; but the two groups of pioneers, quite unconsciously for the most part, tended to emphasize different, in some ways even mutually incompatible, aspects of the democratic ideal. This basic difference in the two frontier legacies was first clearly indicated by an American visitor to Australia, Carter Goodrich, who wrote in *The Economic Record* (November, 1928, pp. 206-207), "Certainly the United States owes its individualism largely to its small man's frontier; I think it is not fanciful to suggest that Australia owes much of its collectivism to the fact that its frontier was hospitable to the large man instead."

[2] For this and for a comparison of the Australian and American frontiers generally, see Russel Ward, *The Australian Legend* (Melbourne, 1958), chap. 9.

We have already stressed the sparseness of Australia's inland population, a condition of affairs springing partly from the land's remoteness from the old world and partly from its aridity. On the one hand the sheer loneliness of Australian bushmen placed a high premium on mutual aid; and on the other it diminished individualistic tendencies by diminishing competition for the land. This trend toward collectivism was accentuated by the fact that in Australia geography, economics, and land legislation, in the first half of the nineteenth century, combined to discourage small-scale agriculture and to encourage large-scale grazing. And from the very beginning the convict system required heavy emphasis on central government control and even on a sort of state-controlled economic collectivism. In the United States, at least up until about 1870 when settlement reached the eastern edge of the great trans-Mississippi plains, the typical frontiersman was a farmer, working his own land with the help of his family and perhaps of a hired hand or two at harvest time. Moreover ample rainfall, fertile soil, and relatively ready access to markets for his produce supported his belief that he could become "independent," if not always rich, by enterprise, thrift, and hard work. In Australia on the other hand aridity, distance from markets, poor communications, and backward farming methods combined to frustrate the petty agriculturist. Sheep, however, could thrive on the native grasses—given a large enough area to graze over—and walk to the coastal markets. Their wool was so much more valuable by weight than grain that it could be carted profitably, if tediously, over many hundreds of miles of rough bush tracks. Thus large-scale pastoralism became the staple industry of the Australian inland. A sheep- or cattle-station, covering perhaps more than a hundred square miles, requires only one resident owner or manager but many working hands. Since most station work—like shearing, droving, or dam-sinking—is seasonal or casual in character, bush-workers received little encouragement to identify their interests with those of their employers. In the 1870's the English novelist, Anthony Trollope, one of whose sons was an Australian station owner, could still write of bush-workers:

> The bulk of the labour is performed by a nomad tribe, who wander in quest of work, and are hired only for a time. . . . the squatter seldom knows whether the man he employs be married or single. They come and go, and are known by queer nicknames or are known by no names at all.[3]

Thus the typical Australian frontiersman was not a self-employed farmer, but a landless, itinerant laborer who had little real chance of

[3] *Australia and New Zealand* (Melbourne, 1876), p. 69.

becoming "independent"—in the financial sense—and who very generally believed himself to have "Buckley's." For him, freedom to climb to the top of the ladder by his own efforts meant less than freedom to combine with his mates against government restrictions (as the convicts had done), against "those wealthy squatters," and indeed against the overwhelming loneliness which quite often rendered insane habitually solitary bushmen who were known as "hatters." Broadly we may say that frontier life evoked similar responses in the two continents, if we remember the very large qualification that it tended to foster collectivist attitudes in Australia almost as strongly as it fostered individualistic ones in North America. With this background in mind, let us return to the squatting rush.

Assimilation to Environment

When transportation to the mainland ceased in 1840 the movement inland was already in full swing, but the deep-seated emancipist-exclusionist dichotomy of the population broke down only gradually. In the last chapter we noticed that the great majority of native-born Australians in the early years sprang mainly from the convict and emancipist classes. Here we must stress that this group—convict, emancipist, and currency people—were the first (white) Australians, in the sense that they first came to think of themselves as such, and to feel strongly that they belonged to the country as it did to them. By and large they had less reason to love Britain than did well-to-do exclusionists. Most of them had not sufficient education to read English magazines, to write letters to relatives, or to keep up other connections with "Home." Nor could they afford to send their children there to be educated, or to return there temporarily or permanently themselves, even if they had wished to do so. The wealthier and more cultivated colonists, on the other hand, for long tended to regard themselves as temporarily exiled Britons. The pattern of these contrasting attitudes was indicated by Watkin Tench, captain of Marines in the First Fleet. In 1791 he wrote of the time when:

> the hour of departure to England, for the marine battalion, drew nigh. If I be allowed to speak from my own feelings on the occasion, I will not say that we contemplated its approach with mingled sensations:— we hailed it with rapture and exultation . . . [Yet] three corporals, one drummer, and 59 privates, accepted of grants of land, to settle at Norfolk Island and Rose Hill . . . [the] majority of them . . . from infatuated affection to female convicts, whose character and habits of life, I am sorry to say, promise from a connection neither honour nor tranquility.[4]

[4] *Narrative of the Expedition to Botany Bay etc.*, reprinted as *Sydney's First Four Years*, ed. L. F. Fitzhardinge (Sydney, 1961), p. 245.

These "other ranks" could, of course, like Tench and his fellow officers, have returned to Britain with free passages and on full pay. Convicts, emancipists, and currency people could not. Naturally they felt, as a rule, even more firmly attached to the new land. In 1837 James Macarthur complained that these people believed "that the colony was *theirs by right*, and that the emigrant settlers were interlopers upon the soil": and in 1843 John Hood wrote in his *Australia and the East* (p. 163):

> The fact of being a drunkard, or a convict, is not looked upon in this country, amongst the *class*, as any disgrace; on the contrary . . . no shame whatever is evinced by the very best amongst them; and they look upon all "self-imported devils" as beneath them, and not worth consideration.

Because the emancipist-currency group constituted the great majority of all colonists in the early days, and because they were also the oldest and most thoroughly acclimatized settlers, many free immigrants of working-class background tended rapidly to assimilate their attitudes.

Many of these ordinary colonists, feeling themselves thoroughly at home in Australia, naturally joined enthusiastically in the squatting rush to the interior. Because of the loneliness, dangers, and hardships associated with it, bush work was easier to get and better paid than work in the cities and towns. As in the United States and other colonies of settlement, newly arrived immigrants tended to prefer life in the relatively "Home-like" cities where they disembarked from Europe; but the bush held few terrors for the old hands and the native born. Census figures show that, in the decade 1841-1851, the proportion of emancipist and currency people in the population increased directly with distance from Sydney. If we consider convicts, emancipists, and native-born persons as one single group and *all* free immigrants as the other, then the ratio of the first to the second in the County of Cumberland during this decade was about one to one. Cumberland was the first-settled area, extending for a radius of about twenty-five or more miles north, east, and south of Sydney. Within the nineteen counties (excluding Cumberland) the proportion was about two to one; and beyond them, that is to say in what were sometimes known as "the squatting districts" beyond the erstwhile "limits of location," more than two hundred and fifty miles from the capital, the proportion was about two-and-a-half to one. Thus the "old Australians," if we may for convenience so call this majority group of mainly lower class people, tended to concentrate disproportionately on the frontier where conditions were such as to accentuate the distinctive, leveling, nationalist attitudes they had already begun to develop.

The situation was neatly reflected in literature and the arts. Until the 1880's writers and painters naturally described the life around them in terms of traditional English literary and artistic conventions, and with a cultivated English audience in mind. The result was that formal literature, even when produced by a really talented native-born son of emancipist parents like Charles Harpur, tended to be little more than a slightly anemic, provincial reflection of its English exemplar. In Harpur's poetry the setting and the intention are usually Australian, but little else. Quite often native authors felt impelled to write about English life, of which they knew nothing at first hand, just as the American Fenimore Cooper did in his first novel before turning, in *The Pioneers* (1823), to the frontier theme. Meanwhile the "old Australians," being largely illiterate, produced little or no formal literature; but they did create directly from the raw life around them a considerable body of folk ballads, songs, and tales which circulated orally. Enough of these survive to show that the people who composed them had already become spiritually Australianized long before 1851, in a way and to a degree that most of the cultured minority had not. Here, for instance, is the oldest extant chorus of one of the most popular bush songs of the first half of the nineteenth century, "The Old Bullock Dray." Stores were taken up-country to the stations, and wool back to Sydney for export, on ponderous two-wheeled bullock-drays the drivers of which were almost always old hands or native-born Australians. The chorus emphasizes the pride of these men in their familiarity with, and mastery of, the frontier environment. At the same time it underlines one of the most important functions of these folk songs, that of assisting acclimatization by clothing an initially strange environment and way of life with the familiar garments of home-spun myth.

So it's roll up your blankets, and let's make a push,
I'll take you up the country and show you the bush;
I'll take you round the stations and learn you how to ride,
And I'll show you how to muster when we cross th' Great Divide!

It is instructive to set against this a stanza from another bullockies' song, reported by a contemporary immigrant litterateur, Frank Fowler. Addressing his English audience Fowler wrote condescendingly of Australian reality:

These bullock-songs are uncouth snatches generally improvised by the drivers themselves, but not destitute of a wild runic poetry, as the following verses from one of them will show:

Olle! Heigh ho!
Blow your horns, blow,
Blow the Southern Cross down if you will;
But on you must go,
Where the fresh gullies flow,
And the thirsty crane wets his red bill.[5]

Comparison with all other extant "uncouth snatches" makes it appallingly probable that Fowler himself provided what he considered to be the touch of "wild runic poetry" in this stanza.

The same dichotomy between educated persons, with one eye cocked over their shoulders toward Europe, and the masses existed in the United States and other "new countries." Thus in 1839 an acute German traveler, Francis J. Grund, wrote of the Great Republic:

"And I can assure you," said I, "that in my own heart I have a much higher respect for the common American, who, in his conduct towards strangers, is solely guided by his own rude notion of dignity, than for the *educated gentleman*, who measures everything, and himself into the bargain, by the standard of another country."

"Agreed! agreed!" cried my two companions; "for the one, however barbarous, has within him the elements of a national character; while the other, however civilised, is but a mutilated European." [6]

We have seen that in 1839 Grund's remarks would have been at least equally applicable to Australia.

Nevertheless the exclusionist-emancipist dichotomy was diminishing at this time, and for masters and men alike the acclimatization process tended to proceed most rapidly on the frontier. In some districts many of the flock masters were emancipists or currency lads who, by superior luck, hard work, sobriety, or skill in "cattle-duffing," had amassed sufficient capital to stock a "run." In nearly all areas there were a few such squatters: but overall, the majority were free immigrants possessing at least a modicum of education and taste, as well as capital. Some were retired army and navy officers from the old country, and not a few were men of real birth and breeding. Most of these immigrant squatters frankly intended to stay in the barbarous wilderness only long enough to make their fortunes before returning to England to live in comfort and refinement: but as the long years of "roughing it" on the pioneering frontier passed, many of them found to their surprise that they too were becoming Australians. One such was Patrick Leslie, pioneer squatter of the Darling Downs.

[5] *Southern Lights and Shadows* etc. (London, 1859), p. 107ff.
[6] Francis J. Grund, *Aristocracy in America* (New York, 1959), p. 30.

Queensland Again

Scottish-born like so many of the early pastoralists, Leslie was twenty years of age when he landed in Sydney in 1835. He went to stay with John Macarthur's nephew, Hannibal, whose daughter he married a few years later. In 1840 he left the last New England out-stations behind him to the south and found rich new country on the western slopes of the Great Divide a hundred miles or two inland from the Moreton Bay penal settlement. He became a successful squatter and, as an elected member of the New South Wales Legislative Assembly, did much to secure the separation of Queensland in 1859 —despite differences on other issues with Dr. Lang, whom he casti-gated as "the Reverend Republican." Having made a reasonable for-tune, he returned to Scotland but then went to New Zealand for some years. In 1878, however, he returned to Australia and died in Sydney. Living the frontier life, many such men came to know and love, not only the land of their adoption, but also those who had already claimed it for their own. Especially in up-country districts free immigrants and old hands came increasingly to know and respect each other, and to share many implicit attitudes to life, even if they seldom at this time came to share each other's manners and modes of pronouncing the English language. Of his pioneering journey to the Darling Downs Leslie wrote afterwards: "We had twenty-two men, all ticket-of-leave or convicts, as good and game a lot of men as ever existed, and who never occasioned us a moment's trouble: worth any forty men I have ever seen since." Of his twenty-two old hands it is recorded that their feelings toward Leslie were such that they swore they would "follow him to hell itself." [7]

We are now in a better position to see why men in the 1880's and since have tended to think of Queensland as the most characteristi-cally Australian of all the colonies. South and Western Australia were settled long after the mother colony of New South Wales, and by free immigrants fresh from Great Britain. Victoria it is true was, like Queensland, first unofficially occupied by squatters and old hands from New South Wales (and Van Diemen's Land); but, by Aus-tralian standards, Victoria occupies only a very small area of well-watered land. This colony was too rich and too cramped for space to remain for long a predominantly pastoral frontier area. Queensland, on the other hand, was the biggest of all the colonies except Western Australia. Most of its land was and remains suitable, but not *too* suit-able, for pastoral occupation. As we have seen, it was first settled by convicts and then by graziers and old hands from the mother colony

[7] H. S. Russell, *The Genesis of Queensland* (Sydney, 1888), pp. 166, 171.

who had already undergone an intensive course of assimilation to Australian conditions. It was, and to a considerable extent has remained, the frontier colony—or state. Climate, as well as area and the accident of late settlement, may have something to do with it. If, compared with Britain, all Australia is hot and dry, Queensland is the hottest and driest part of the continent to be occupied—except on the coast, where it is the hottest and wettest. If characteristically Australian habits and attitudes are apprehended as those which differ most from traditional British ones, we have seen that such reactions were evoked most completely by frontier conditions: and for geographic reasons the traditional Australian tribulations of frontier life —bushfires, droughts, dust storms, floods, poisonous snakes, sharks, and insect plagues—prevail in Queensland more than in any other colony. Besides, on the coastal plain Queenslanders grow sugar cane from which they distill rum for the Commonwealth. Perhaps it is the heat which causes them to drink rather more than their share of it. Certainly the heat has made it much more difficult for them to preserve formal English styles of dress and behavior. In North Queensland only the most determinedly respectable burghers wear coats in the street. As a visiting Englishman wrote in 1886, "The Englishman in Queensland is, like the sheep, developing into a different species."

By the mid-century transportation had been, or in Van Diemen's Land was on the verge of being, abolished, except in the isolated western colony where it was just beginning. Legislative Councils in New South Wales, Victoria, South Australia, and Van Diemen's Land had been invited to devise more fully representative constitutions for approval by the Imperial Parliament. Except in the frontier area, which was to become the separate colony of Queensland in 1859, most of the best pastoral land had been occupied, if thinly, by the "shepherd kings" and the "nomad tribe" of bush-workers who were, in an important sense, the first Australians. The pastoral boom had also drawn from Britain an increasing stream of free immigrants, some of whom were men of substance and culture. The old antagonism between the emancipist and exclusionist factions was diminishing as men in both groups, but especially the former, began to feel at home in the land; yet the colonial middle class had barely come into existence. Retail trade and secondary industry had achieved only a rudimentary stage of development. Even Sydney was still not very much more than an entrepôt center, siphoning rum and other station stores into, and wool out of, the interior. About 150,000 convicts had been transported, but the total white population of Australia was still only 405,356 in 1851. The discovery of gold in that year led, not so much to changes in, as to a rapid acceleration of, existing trends.

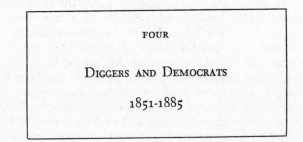

On 12 February 1851 gold was discovered in Summerhill Creek on the western slopes of the Blue Mountains. Fear of convictism may have had some influence in suppressing news of earlier finds, but by 1851 Australian society had become so open that suppressing the news of Edward Hargraves' discovery would no longer have been practicable. Besides, the gold rush to California in 1849 had enticed away a disquietingly large number of the more enterprising Australian colonists. The rush to the Turon (New South Wales) diggings had scarcely gathered momentum when the newly separated Victorian government offered a reward for the discovery of a payable goldfield in its territory. Before the end of the year it was obvious that the Victorian fields near Ballarat were even richer than those of the mother colony.

Eureka Stockade

The immediate impact of the discoveries on the placid pastoral society was so great that, for a time, some officials feared the breakdown of social order. Shepherds and other employees, in both country and town, left their jobs en masse for the diggings. The draconic provisions of the Masters and Servants acts availed little when so many police constables and other civil servants followed—not to arrest the absconders, but to join them. Governmental difficulties increased from September, 1852, when the tidal wave of overseas goldseekers broke on Melbourne. Thousands of deserting sailors joined the eager "new chums" in their precipitate trek to the goldfields. Nevertheless civil order did not break down. Except for the shortlived Eureka revolt at Ballarat in December 1854, there were few considerable riots and, by Californian standards, a surprising absence of lynch-law and other disorders. Contemporary observers nearly all agreed on the high level of self-discipline and responsibility among the diggers. The goldfields entertainer and satirist, Charles Thatcher, for instance, wrote of "the inevitable double-barrelled gun, as if gold was a thing to be shot at and brought down . . . [as the chief among the] other useless trifles [and] usual treasures of a new chum." The adjutant-general of New South Wales, Lieutenant-Colonel Godfrey Charles Mundy, who left for Britain in August 1851, wrote sensibly of the reasons for the relatively orderly life on the fields. In contrast to the Californian situation, he pointed out, gold had been found in areas adjacent to seats of firmly established government, the vast majority of diggers belonged to one national stock—the British, and there was no warlike aboriginal race and no large bodies of foreigners to cause friction by upsetting traditionally accepted mores. Yet we should not exaggerate the effect of these stabilizing factors. The sudden strain on the colonial administrations did result in the only considerably bloody riot in Australia's history.

By 1854 most of the alluvial surface gold had been won. In 1852 the approximate value of gold found per head of population in the Victorian fields was £390. This figure fell to £240 in 1853, and £148 in 1854.[1] All but the luckiest diggers began to find paying the miner's monthly licence fee of thirty shillings irksome. Much more provocative, in the opinion of the diggers, was the inefficient yet brutal way in which the police collected the tax. A tradition of unusually intense hostility between policemen and populace stemmed from convict days, and the "Russian sort of way" in which uniformed, mounted police often rode after diggers in "licence hunts" did nothing to lessen the bitterness. As discontent with these very tangible evils grew among all diggers, some of their leaders began speaking of "no taxation without representation" and demanding far-reaching political reforms, including those of the People's Charter which had been drawn up in Britain in 1838—universal manhood suffrage, vote by ballot, equal electoral districts, annual elections of parliament, abolition of property qualifications, and payment of members. In the last weeks of 1854 the Ballarat Reform League began to organize revolt. Led by an educated, middle-class Irishman, Peter Lalor, the diggers took up arms and built a stockade just outside Ballarat on a hilltop commanding the road to Melbourne. The stockade's defenders then proclaimed the Republic of Victoria, hoisted a blue-and-white Southern Cross flag, and swore by it "to stand truly by each other, and fight to defend [their] rights and liberties." Thirst was their undoing. On Saturday 2 December most of the armed diggers sallied forth to the hotels as usual. Troops and police attacked at 4:30 on Sunday morning in the half light of dawn, and in a few minutes Eureka Stockade had fallen. Twenty-two diggers and six soldiers were killed in the

[1] Geoffrey Serle, *The Golden Age* (Melbourne, 1963), p. 86.

fight or died later of wounds. Among the dead diggers ten were natives of Ireland, two of Germany, two of Canada, one of England, one
of Scotland, and one of Australia. Two of the remaining five were
named Crowe and Fenton but their birthplaces are unknown. All we
know of the last three is that one of them was usually known on the
Eureka by the nickname of "Happy Jack." Lalor, who lost an arm in
the fight, and a number of other alleged ring leaders were soon apprehended by the authorities. Among them were some Americans, but
their consul in Melbourne succeeded in having all save one of them
released before the trial. The exception was an American Negro
named John Joseph about whom the consul does not seem to have
concerned himself. He was one of the thirteen men brought to trial
for high treason, but public opinion was so overwhelmingly in favor
of the diggers that the jury acquitted them. Lalor lived to become the
Speaker of the Victorian Legislative Assembly.

Ever since 1854 Australians have argued about the significance of
Eureka. In the last century popular opinion saw it as a fight for liberty, small in scale but great in symbolic significance, which hastened
the establishment of full responsible self-government in 1856. This
view was reflected by Mark Twain, who wrote in his *More Tramps
Abroad* (1875) that Eureka was "the finest thing in Australasian
history. . . . It was the barons and John over again. . . . It was
Concord and Lexington . . . another instance of a victory won by a
lost battle." Conservatives tended to dismiss it as a local riot, inspired
by Irish and foreign malcontents, which had no appreciable effect on
events at large. In this century historians have continued the debate,
sometimes with acrimony. In 1923, long after most of the participants
were dead, a Ballarat citizens' committee erected a monument to
mark the site of the only battle fought on Australian soil. The
memorial's inscription reflects nicely the uneasily ambivalent Australian attitude toward the Eureka Stockade: "To the honoured memory
of the heroic pioneers who fought and fell, on this sacred spot, in the
cause of liberty, and the soldiers who fell at Duty's call." Similarly
the bullet-torn insurgent flag is still preserved in the Ballarat Art Gallery, not however in a prominently placed display case, but under lock
and key in the curator's private desk. No commemorative postage
stamp was issued by the Liberal Government of the Commonwealth
in 1954.

Chinese and American Diggers

Most witnesses before the Royal Commission which inquired into
the causes of the Eureka revolt felt that the diggers would have resorted to arms even if no foreigners had been among them. However

this may be, there is general agreement among historians that the so-called "white Australia policy" stems from passions aroused by the presence of foreigners on the goldfields. Before 1851 evidence suggests that there was relatively little race prejudice among the colonists.[2] After the gold-rush decade racist attitudes, and legislation aimed at excluding colored people, continued to increase until they were given continent-wide force by the Commonwealth Immigration Restriction Act of 1901. Yet, as we have seen, the influence of foreigners during the decade has often been exaggerated. The vast majority of immigrants continued to come from the British Isles, and a great many of them brought wives and children with them. In 1862 92.5 per cent of the whole population had been born in the British Isles or in Australia. Most of the alien gold-seekers came without dependents, and many of them left after a few years on the diggings. Most of those who stayed were assimilated into the Australian society almost as readily and rapidly as the newcomers from Britain; but this was emphatically not the case with the Chinese, who comprised at once the largest group of foreign nationals and the only considerable non-European one. In 1857 in the colony of Victoria about one in every seven adult males was a Chinese.

The Chinese seem on the whole to have been singularly law-abiding and inoffensive people. They were conspicuous by their absence at Eureka, and not even the most prejudiced colonists ever imagined the existence of a Chinese conspiracy to seize power. It was rather—as with the Australian aborigines—that their very meekness was their undoing. Nearly all were of the coolie class, imported in the first instance by a few of their wealthy compatriots to work for their keep and for little else. Generally they kept to themselves on the goldfields, only venturing to work "tailings" on claims that had been dug over and deserted by Europeans. Later many took up occupations such as market-gardening and laundering which were disdained by most colonists. Yet their low standard of living, their strange appearance and manners, and their completely alien culture aroused distrust which, by guilt reaction in the minds of the white majority, soon became hatred. People did not fear them, but feared that more and more would come to live in Australia until they became the majority when, naturally, they might do as they had been done by.

Germans and Americans made up the next largest alien groups among the gold-rush immigrants, though they were very few in num-

---

[2] For this and following references in this chapter to racism in Australia, see Russel Ward, "An Australian Legend: an Historical View of the White Australia Policy," in *Royal Australian Historical Society, Journal and Proceedings* (Sydney), Vol. 47, Part 6, 1961.

ber compared with the Chinese. In 1857 there were only about 4,000 or 5,000 Americans in Victoria compared with about 40,000 Orientals. Yet the former exercised on Australian life an influence out of all proportion to their numbers. Many of them came from the Californian goldfields and their very similar frontier outlook, their more colorful "go-ahead" ways, and their democratic republican background appealed strongly to colonists standing impatiently on the threshold of self-government. There is evidence to suggest that some American diggers, bringing with them their pre-Civil War racist attitudes, had an appreciable influence on the growth of color-prejudice in Australia. The two major anti-Chinese riots on Victorian goldfields, at Bendigo in 1854 and on the Buckland diggings in 1857, took place on the fourth of July, the anniversary of the American Declaration of Independence. At the Hanging Rock goldfield in Northern New South Wales another riot marked the "Glorious Fourth" in 1852, because a party of seven Americans "had a notion to Lynch [the Chinese]."

Americans also took a leading part in revolutionizing land transport at this time. Before 1851 four-wheeled vehicles had been almost unknown in Australia outside the capital cities—and not very common even in Sydney. In the bush men traveled on horseback, or else plodded along on foot beside the ponderous two-wheeled bullock-drays which carried all stores into, and wool out of, the interior of the country. There were practically no roads, and bush tracks were held to be impassable by four-wheeled vehicles. In 1851 and 1852 most of the newly arrived gold-seekers walked the hundred or so miles from Sydney or Melbourne to the diggings, but from 1853 onward most rode in the new, fast coaches. Freeman Cobb and James Rutherford, two newly arrived Americans, had most to do with the transformation. Despite the gloomy forebodings of the old colonial hands, the sturdily built, four-wheeled, Yankee-style coaches proved quite capable of negotiating bush tracks. With five stops to change horses, they carried passengers and mails up to eighty miles in a day, as against the bullock-dray's performance of as many miles in a week—under favorable conditions. Cobb and Co. began operating their coaching service between Melbourne and the main Victorian goldfield towns like Ballarat and Bendigo. By 1870 in the three eastern mainland colonies the company was harnessing 6,000 horses every day; its coaches were covering about 28,000 miles per week, and it was drawing about £100,000 a year in mail subsidies from the colonial governments. For more than half a century in Australia the name "Cobb and Co." was almost synonymous with "inland travel," although Cobb himself sold out early. He returned to America, became for a time state senator in the Massachusetts legislature, and then went to South Africa in 1870 to build another coaching empire, but died there three years later.

Results of the Gold Rush

It is now time to ask what broad effects the gold rush had on Australian history. Most obviously it caused a sudden increase in population and wealth. In the sixty odd years after the First Fleeters landed at Sydney Cove the population increased slowly to 405,000. In the decade of the Gold Rush, 1851-1861, this figure grew to about 1,146,-000. In these ten years the white population of the continent nearly trebled, while that of the infant colony of Victoria increased six-fold from 87,000 to 540,000. For the next forty years or so Victoria, and not the mother colony of New South Wales, was the most prosperous and influential colony. National wealth and the gross value of exports increased proportionately during the decade. Naturally most contemporaries thought that it was scarcely possible to exaggerate the importance and the likely results of the discoveries. Most seem to have felt that W. C. Wentworth was uttering only a truism when in July 1851 he said that gold had opened a new era "which must in a very few years precipitate us from a colony into a nation." Yet ten years later many men doubted whether the golden decade had made very much difference to Australian society. In 1861 the first principal of Sydney University, John Woolley, gave a public lecture in which he painted a somewhat idealized picture of the cultural and national unity of ancient Greece. He then asked:

> Can we hope that Australia in a hundred years will present a counterpart to this picture? Five years ago [i.e., at the time of the inauguration of responsible government] we should have answered with an indignant and enthusiastic affirmative. But experience has taught us humility; we have learned that no accidental impulse can precipitate an infant community into a nation. . . . A corporate like a national body grows only from within.[3]

Historians have tended to echo these conflicting opinions but with a time lag of a century or so. Many were motivated by a conscious or unconscious desire to minimize the influence of Australia's convict origins. Until quite recently most writers exaggerated the revolutionary effects of gold. Some even spoke at times of the "second" or "real" foundation of Australia in 1851. Now the wheel has come full circle, and most historians would probably endorse I. D. McNaughtan's words in Gordon Greenwood's *Australia* (1955):

[3] *Schools of Arts and Colonial Nationality: a Lecture etc.* (Sydney, 1861).

With the perspective of a century it can be seen that the diggers' era left a fainter impress on Australian life than the first ten years of the squatting age . . . [1832-1842] . . . Gold . . . gave a greater complexity to Australian society and a powerful impulse to existing trends. . . . Certainly it did not create a nation. The Colonies had before them another generation of parochialism and hard pioneering before political, economic and social life began to set in the native and characteristic forms of modern Australia.

There is something in both views. If the gold discoveries did no more than accelerate most existing trends, the degree to which some of them were speeded up was immense. On the other hand gold actually slowed down, or masked for a generation, the development of other trends—most notably of an indigenous national sentiment. Both effects stemmed largely from the very marked growth of middle-class influence brought about by the gold rush.

We have seen that, with the cessation of transportation to the eastern mainland in 1840, thousands of assisted migrants were brought out to supply the labor market. The pastoral boom attracted also a much smaller number of aspiring squatters, many of whom were men of substance and culture. Yet in an almost purely pastoral economy the number and influence of city-dwelling, middle-class, professional people remained relatively slight—certainly by subsequent Australian standards. There was no doubt an element of exaggeration in the 1851 *Remonstrance of the Legislative Council of New South Wales*, addressed to the Home government, which roundly declared that the majority of the assisted immigrants were the spiritless "outpourings of the poor-houses and the unions of the United Kingdom": but until that year most observers endorsed James Dixon's opinion that Australia was "a country possessing two distinct sorts of mankind. . . . Perhaps in all societies it is in some measure the same, but here it is more strongly felt." [4] Gold rapidly changed this state of affairs. The major colonial governments suspended, or greatly reduced, their assisted immigration programs as it became clear that thousands of migrants, able and anxious to pay for their own voyages, were crowding Australia-bound ships. Most of those who arrived during the golden decade had at least enough money to pay the high fares demanded, and there is certainly something in the view that they were usually much more self-reliant and enterprising people on landing than the earlier immigrants had been. It seems too that they included a lower proportion of unskilled laborers and a correspondingly higher proportion of skilled and semiskilled artisans, tradesmen, white-collar workers, and professional men. Unquestionably the new-chum gold-

---

[4] *Narrative of a Voyage to New South Wales etc.* (London, 1822), p. 92.

seekers, after their often quite short sojourn on the diggings, helped to raise the general standard of education, refinement, and culture. The University of Sydney, for instance, was founded in 1852 and the Australian Museum in the same city in the following year. Melbourne opened its university in 1854 and its great Public Library in 1856. Universities opened their doors also in Adelaide and Hobart before 1891. In this same period following the gold discoveries art galleries and libraries were begun in the colonial capitals. Churches established most of the large private boarding and day schools—still probably in some respects the best, as well as the most fashionable, secondary schools in the country. Lord mayors and aldermen symbolized their faith in progress by building in stone ornate, Victorian-Gothic city halls—usually both more commodious and more inconvenient than anything of the kind erected since. It is important to remember, however, that the cultural aspirations of the period were considerably more grandiose than its cultural achievement was impressive. For the thirty or forty years following 1851, even in many ways until the end of World War Two, Australia remained basically a remote, provincial British society. In some ways its British character was actually accentuated, at least temporarily, and especially in Victoria and in the cities, by the effects of the gold rush.

This was so for two reasons. First, the sudden influx of British immigrants greatly increased the already high proportion which was in fact British by birth and nurture, as well as by sentiment. Second, the high proportion of middle-class people among the newcomers greatly increased that respectable section of Australian society which, as we have seen, always tends to look to the mother country—naturally the source of culture and civilization—for its inspiration. Yet this does not mean that the new immigrants exercised a conservative political influence. Quite the contrary—unless we equate conservatism with stability rather than with preservation of the *status quo*. On the whole they seem to have had a stabilizing effect on colonial life precisely because most of them were liberal or radical in outlook. There were, after all, very few immigrants of aristocratic or upper class (in a contemporary English sense) background among the newcomers. These few were often labeled by the colonists "remittance men" or "broken-down swells." Few of the artisans, white-collar people, and tradesmen who made up the majority dreamed of entertaining socialist or revolutionary notions. As Peter Lalor said in a well-known speech, "I would ask these gentlemen what they mean by the term 'Democracy.' Do they mean Chartism or Communism or Republicanism? If so, I never was, I am not now, nor do I ever intend to be, a Democrat." Lalor's speech was made after, not before, the Eureka affair and it certainly plays down the extent of Chartist influence among the diggers. Even so, most of them seem to have belonged to that middling, if rising, order of contemporary British society which made Mr. Gladstone such a power at the time in England. As Sir Charles Dilke said of the period, Australian society was English "with the upper class left out." Thus, in the third quarter of the nineteenth century Australian political sentiment was overwhelmingly liberal, even radical, but at the same time strongly individualist and not markedly either collectivist or nationalist. John Stuart Mill was the philosophical mentor of most politicians literate enough to be aware of theoretical writings.

Establishment of Responsible Government

We have seen that the Imperial Parliament had passed an Act for the Better Government of her Majesty's Australian Colonies in 1850, even before the gold discoveries. This act gave to the then four major colonies (New South Wales, Van Diemen's Land, Victoria, and South Australia) legislative councils, two-thirds elective on the New South Wales model; but it also extended the franchise on which they were to be elected, and invited them to submit for imperial approval constitutions of their own devising, subject only to the provisos that final control of Crown lands and of the civil services were to remain in the hands of the imperial government. In New South Wales W. C. Wentworth, who had grown steadily more conservative with the years, chaired the Council's committee of constitution-makers, which included also James Macarthur. As leader of the squatters, Wentworth's voice was loudest in demanding that the new colonial legislatures should control fully the disposal of Crown lands and all colonial revenue including the civil lists; but at the same time he sought to ensure that the new parliaments would themselves be controlled by the great propertied "interests" of the colonies—primarily, that is, by the squatters. The demand for full responsible self-government was quickly conceded by the secretary of state for the colonies, in large part because, as he wrote in a dispatch of 1852, the gold discoveries had "imparted new and unforeseen features to [Australia's] political and social condition." The lingering aroma of convictism was no longer deemed a sufficient reason for refusing to the Australian colonies what had already been granted, following the Durham Report of 1839, to the major North American colonies and was in process of being granted to New Zealand.

The other constitutional recommendations of the Council's Select Committee provoked determined local opposition. Wentworth, Macarthur, and their supporters sought conservative safeguards, including the creation of an upper house consisting of an order of hereditary colonial baronets, electoral arrangements which would give the squatting districts grossly disproportionate representation in the lower house, and a provision that the constitution could never be altered except by an "unusual majority" of two-thirds of the members of both houses. The first proposal for an hereditary aristocracy was so to speak laughed out of court, partly as the result of a speech by Daniel Deniehy, a twenty-four-year-old currency lad of convict stock who might have made a bigger mark in the world if he had not drunk himself to death a few years later. He suggested that in the proposed "bunyip aristocracy" James Macarthur would become at least an earl, and offered as the coat-of-arms for his family "a field vert, and emblazoned on this field . . . a rum keg of a New South Wales order of chivalry." [5] In the event New South Wales acquired an upper house whose members were nominated—for life terms—by the governor, but in the other three colonies upper house members were elected on a moderately restrictive property qualification. Ironically, these elected upper houses have proved on the whole more effective in resisting change than the nominated houses in New South Wales and Queensland. Indeed we have seen that the latter state abolished its legislative council in 1922. Like Nebraska it seems to be no worse governed with only one house than its neighbors with two. The other major safeguard of propertied interests, the two-thirds majority clause, was defeated in Great Britain. When the New South Wales Constitution Bill came before the House of Commons, Lord John Russell, the architect of the British Great Reform Bill of 1832, was serving as colonial secretary. His influence may have been instrumental in having the bill altered so as to allow for constitutional amendment by a simple majority. Wentworth was dismayed at this opening of the flood-gates to the influence of "mere population . . . , selfishness, ignorance and democracy." The old patriot returned only briefly to the scene of his triumphs, now saddled, as he saw it, with "a Yankee constitution." He retired in 1862 to live in England and died there ten years later.

Thus in the years 1855 and 1856 the four major colonies achieved —or were given—almost complete control of their own destinies. Queensland was granted a similar constitution upon its separation from New South Wales four years later, but Western Australia, which was still receiving convicts, had to wait until 1890, long after its convict period was over. Some of Wentworth's forebodings were

<hr>

[5] Quoted C. M. H. Clark, *Select Documents in Australian History 1851-1900* (Sydney, 1955), p. 341. The bunyip was a mythical monster, believed by some Aborigines to haunt swamps and lagoons.

fulfilled with what seemed, to many contemporaries, astonishing rapidity. By the end of 1858 the three most populous colonies of Victoria, New South Wales, and South Australia had established constitutions which were among the most democratic then existing in the world. South Australia led the way. Its first responsible Parliament was elected in 1856 on universal manhood suffrage and by secret ballot. The latter method of voting is still sometimes called, in Britain and North America, the "Australian ballot." Moreover, about two-thirds of the seats in the lower house, the Legislative Assembly, were given to Adelaide and its immediate neighborhood, and the whole colony voted as a single constituency, on a moderately restrictive property franchise, for the Legislative Council. Thus the influence of "mere population" was given full weight from the beginning. Herman Merivale, the liberal-minded under-secretary of state for the colonies, was intrigued to see how what he saw as perhaps "the only thoroughly Benthamite constitution" in the world would work. Victoria also employed the secret ballot from the beginning. Within two or three years popular pressure on elected representatives had won the secret ballot and almost complete manhood suffrage in New South Wales also. Many contemporaries felt that the Australian colonies had "shot Niagara," and such people looked forward apprehensively with Wentworth to the results of giving political power to "mere numbers." But they were wrong. As Professor C. M. H. Clark has stressed, unobtrusive safeguards for propertied interests were still embedded in the colonial constitutions. Except in South Australia plural voting—for those with property in more than one electorate and for some other presumptively respectable persons—continued until the late 1880's and sometimes longer. Nomadic pastoral workers, of whom there were many, and other men of no fixed address, were excluded from voting at least as long as were women. Payment of members was not introduced until 1870 in Victoria, and not until the late 1880's in the other colonies, and its absence helped effectively to deprive working-class voters of direct representation in parliaments by men drawn from their own ranks. There were other and deeper reasons, however, for the moderate tone of colonial politics from the granting of responsible government until the late 1880's.

Colonial Politics

Some of them have been mentioned already. As we have seen, responsible government might not have been established when it was, if it had not been for the great strengthening of the middle class brought about by the gold discoveries. Moreover, without this middle order of liberal-minded but respectable townspeople, self-governing institutions would probably not have functioned as smoothly as they did. Secondly, the golden windfall brought about a great diversification of the economy. Wool remained king—as it still does; but for the first time retail trades of all kinds flourished, and many rudimentary manufacturing industries such as food-processing, and the making of builders' supplies and of clothes for the local market, were established. Though there were brief periods of recession, until 1891 there was no serious check to the prosperous and steadily expanding colonial economies. Under these conditions skilled workmen, no less than their employers, could aspire to vastly better living standards than obtained in contemporary Britain. Artisans formed trade unions in the cities, and many skilled building workers won for themselves an eight-hour day from 1856 onward in Sydney and Melbourne. But most workers, including almost all rural employees, remained unorganized until the late 1880's, and most of the small craft unions in the towns spent almost as much time on keeping unqualified men out of their ranks as on agitating for better pay and conditions. Many, even of their leaders, held to the conservative belief that trade unions should "keep out of politics." Thus, the colonial parliaments were filled during the period largely by middle-class townspeople. A radical-minded Victorian barrister, George Higinbotham, who was himself a member of Parliament for many years, sardonically characterized contemporary politicians as men drawn for the most part from "the wealthy lower orders . . . lawyers, journalists, officials, publicans and traders of the metropolis." This was so in the first instance because working-class voters, in so far as they were politically conscious, agreed with middle-class businessmen in resenting the traditionally established dominance of affairs by the "pure merino" squatting interest. It continued to be so for thirty years because of the political, social, and economic conditions sketched above. So true was Dilke's dictum that Australian society lacked an "upper class" that, until the Eighties, it is hard to see many signs of the growth of political parties based on fixed principles, or on class, religious, regional, or other interests. From at least 1860 onward nearly all actual or aspiring politicians at least liked to let it be thought that they were "liberals." Men of unusual ability, like Henry Parkes or John Robertson in New South Wales, or Graham Berry in Victoria, tended to attract a band of personal followers which could be held together for brief periods by the conferment of places or perquisites, or of public works in the right electorates: but as every member gloried in his "independence" and felt free to vote on each new issue as his private principles, conscience, or interest dictated, these alliances were usually brief and precarious. The promise of a new railway extension to the member for one constituency, or of a few places in the civil service to the clients of another, might put a governing coalition into or out of office. The result was that governments rose and fell with almost Gallic frequency and that, for most of the period in most of the colonies, parties could be distinguished only as the (temporary) "ministerialists" or "opposition." Thus John Martineau wrote in his *Letters from Australia* (1869: pp. 50, 133):

> It is a fact notorious in Victoria that a proportion of the Legislative Assembly, sufficient to sway its vote on almost any measure, . . . is altogether corrupt and amenable to bribes! . . . In answer to a question as to the character and composition of the [New South Wales] Lower House . . . I was told that it was *now* no worse than that of Victoria.

Yet we should notice that not even this hostile witness claimed that the *majority* of members were altogether corrupt. Some consistently held throughout long parliamentary careers to at least a few general principles, like support for free trade or protectionist fiscal policies, and some naturally proved in office more liberal than others. Though the level of political corruption was, understandably, higher than it became later after payment of members was introduced and fixed parties developed, many members undoubtedly worked conscientiously for the public weal, as they "independently" saw it. During the thirty years or so following 1856 they spent much time wrangling over local developmental questions—"roads and bridges" issues, as they were often called; but even these parish pump arguments usually resulted in added, if piecemeal, development of the country's resources. The politicians also debated and legislated upon three great questions which were agitating their constituents. These were the control and use of the land, the control of education, and the best kind of fiscal policy to be followed. We shall glance at each in turn.

Squatters and Selectors

By the time gold was discovered much of the best and most accessible country had already been occupied by graziers. In the oldest colonies of New South Wales and Van Diemen's Land quite large areas near Sydney, Hobart, and Launceston had been granted as estates in freehold to wealthy settlers like the Macarthurs. Farther out, vast areas were leased by the squatters under easy terms which gave them a "pre-emptive right" to buy the best pockets of country outright. Yet much of this land was well watered and fertile enough to support agriculture. As the gold fever subsided, men asked more and more loudly why so much land should be "locked up" in pastoral leases which supported only a very sparse, and relatively impoverished, human population of shepherds and bushworkers. If the vast sheepwalks were cut up into small blocks and sold to working agricultural proprietors, it was held that an "independent" class of yeomen farmers would, with their families, bring new population and prosperity to the bush. Thus, almost from the beginning of the gold-rush decade, there arose an increasing popular clamor to "unlock the lands," and contention over the land question was the main preoccupation of colonial parliaments for the first ten years or more of responsible government.

Historians used to believe that the free selection acts of 1860 and following years were passed in response to this popular demand. However, recent research by D. W. A. Baker and others[6] has shown that the matter was by no means as simple as this. There were in fact relatively few successful diggers and other small capitalists who yearned to become farmers on their own account. It now seems that the "lawyers, journalists, officials, publicans and traders of the metropolis," and of the country towns, who had no such ambition for themselves, provided most of the movement's impetus. These people, whose numbers had been so mightily augmented by the inrush of new immigrants, resented what they—in common with the rest of the population—saw as the squatting interest's near-monopoly of political and economic power. Thus the cry to "unlock the lands" was not so much the result of genuine land hunger as a popular slogan for uniting all who wished to attack the "privileges" and pretensions of the squatters. Moreover, there were also cogent economic reasons why middle-class townspeople wished to see the countryside populated with self-employed smallholders instead of sheep. In the Fifties and for decades afterward, most squatters spent little money in the country towns near their stations. Generally their drays took the wool clip to the colonial capital each year and carried back flour, tea, sugar, tar, tools, and other station supplies bought from wholesale importing houses near the wharfside. Naturally retail traders, lawyers, doctors, and other professional men tended to believe that their own prosperity would be enhanced by the creation of the "numerous, industrious and virtuous agricultural population" which the Rev. Lang continually advocated. Acts which aimed, or which at least purported to aim, at placing "small men" on the land were passed by the New South Wales Parliament in 1861. They were piloted through

⁶ "The Origins of Robertson's Land Acts," in *Historical Studies: Australia and New Zealand* (Melbourne), May 1958, and G. A. Price, *Genesis of the Robertson Land Acts of 1861: A Study of the Evidence in the Liverpool Plains* (Univ. New England, M.A. thesis, 1963).

the House by the secretary for lands, John (later Sir John) Robertson, who was himself a squatter and also the owner of considerable freehold land. A folk song of the day celebrated, somewhat prematurely as it turned out, the popular triumph.

> Come all you Cornstalks the victory's won,
> John Robertson's triumphed, the lean days are gone!
> No more through the bush we'll go humping the drum,
> For the Land Bill has passed and the good times have come.
>
> No more through the bush with our swags need we roam,
> For to ask of the squatters to give us a home:
> Now the land is unfettered and we may reside
> In a place of our own by some clear waterside.*

The Robertson Acts seemed to rest on the principle that he who would live on and cultivate the land had the first claim to it. Anyone —man, woman or child—could select a block of Crown land for his farm, before it had been surveyed and whether it was part of a pastoral lease or not. The block must be not less than forty nor more than 320 acres in extent. The selector had to pay a deposit of five shillings an acre to receive his right to occupancy, and the remaining fifteen shillings per acre were supposed to be paid within three years. He had also to live on the selection for at least one year and "improve" it to the value of at least £1 an acre to receive his freehold title to the land. At the same time the acts sought to protect the squatters' equity in their leaseholds and to give them some protection from too many genuine selectors or from blackmailing speculators. The squatter was given, for instance, a preemptive right to one twenty-fifth of his station and to particular areas on which he had built "improvements" such as shearing sheds, dams, or fences. In practice, the acts failed to increase markedly the number of agricultural smallholders in New South Wales. Instead, they had the effect of vastly increasing the amount of freehold land in the hands of big graziers and pastoral companies. In the twenty-two years from 1861 to 1883 29,000,000 acres of Crown land were alienated, but the area under cultivation grew by only about half a million. E. G. Shann summed up in a well-known phrase the general effects of the free selection acts in all colonies: "And so it came to pass that demagogue dispersed the public estate and pastoralists gathered up the freehold thereof."

The reasons for the failure of the land acts have been much can-

---

* "Cornstalks" = native-born Australians, particularly from N. S. W. "Humping the drum" = carrying one's swag—i.e., tramping through the bush with one's bundle of belongings.

vassed. Historians have pointed to the vast amount of sharp practice engaged in by men of all classes, usually within the letter, though not the spirit, of the law. The squatters acquired millions of acres in freehold by "dummying." Wife, children, friends, or permanent employees of a squatter would select on his behalf the best parts of his run in order to keep out selectors. When the "dummy" had obtained full legal title to his selection, ownership was transferred to the squatter. An opposite maneuver was known as "peacocking," an expression apparently derived from the great number of beautiful "eyes" in the tail of a displaying peacock. Small speculators or large "land-sharks" would select the "eyes" or richest parts of a run—with or without the help of dummies—solely in order to force the squatter to buy, at an enhanced price, these well-watered blocks without which the rest of his run was useless. But it is probable that, even if all men had been honest idealists, the land acts would have met with little more success. In the eastern colonies farming techniques were extraordinarily backward at this period. Capital, which most genuine selectors lacked, was just as necessary as a strong back and a stout heart. Most crippling of all was the primitive state of transport. In 1861, for instance, it was still much cheaper to transport a ton of wheat across the Pacific from Valparaiso to Sydney than to carry it about 150 miles by bullock-dray from the vicinity of Goulburn on one of the main bush "roads" of the period. It was not until railways began to crisscross the transmontane wheat-lands in the last decade of the nineteenth century that agriculture became a reasonably stable and expansive industry in New South Wales.

In Victoria, to the accompaniment of much agitation for legislation on the model of the American homesteading acts, three major bills were passed in 1860, 1862, and 1865. These resulted in putting rather more genuine farmers on the land. Between 1861 and 1881 the area under crop increased by about a million acres: but even more land than in New South Wales—relative to the total areas of the two colonies—found its way into the freehold possession of pastoralists. In Queensland, despite the passage of ten land Acts between 1860 and 1884, the results were even less impressive; while in Tasmania, over an even longer period, the amount of cultivated land in the colony remained almost stationary. The effort to settle farmers on the land was successful only in South Australia, but this achievement sprang from the peculiar character of the province's geography and population rather than from any peculiar genius in its politicians. South Australian wheat-lands lay in a compact area near the capital, on a fertile coastal plain blessed by a climate ideal for wheat-growing. The crop could be carted cheaply, over very short distances, to one of a dozen small ports or to Port Adelaide. South Australia's pious farmers worked hard and intelligently. In the 1840's, when other Australian farmers were still reaping their crops by hand, John Ridley and John Wrathall Bull invented a mechanical stripper. Seed drills and stump-jump ploughs were invented in the same colony during the following decades. The latter implement substituted for the conventional ploughshare steel discs, backed by strong springs, which made it possible to cultivate soil from which ground-level stumps and tree roots had not been completely removed. Between 1860 and 1880 South Australia's wheat crop was about equal to that of all the other colonies combined, and she was exporting her surplus to Britain as well as to Sydney and Brisbane.

The selection acts generally failed, then, to accomplish what was ostensibly their prime purpose. Yet we should notice that they— or the struggle around them—did much to achieve what was at least a secondary aim of many who participated in the drawn-out campaign —namely, to transfer the balance of political power to the urban population under the leadership of middle-class business and professional men. Economically, the wool industry continued to be preeminent, although many new industries, both primary and secondary, were growing up in its shadow; and, paradoxically, even wool contributed to the dominance of city interests as banks and finance companies took over the ownership of more and more pastoral properties toward the end of the period. The social prestige of the great pastoral proprietors remained high, as it still does. Their economic power remained great too, but became relatively less. Their domination of the political scene was broken in the first ten years of responsible government. Thereafter, their political influence was exercised more and more indirectly, and on more equal terms with that of other pressure groups in the community.

Free, Compulsory, and Secular Education

The history of education in Australia is very complex, but basically it may be said that most schools might still be under religious control if it had not been for the seemingly irreconcilable differences between different bodies of Christians and even, at times, between those within the same churches. In the early days, the Church of England was naturally the official church but, despite attempts to make it so, it never quite became the established church as in England. The fact that until Governor Darling's time Anglican chaplains were frequently also civil magistrates, who were wont to order floggings no less generously than their lay brethren, strengthened opposition to such a step—among the emancipists naturally, but also among many influential freemen such as the Rev. Lang. Thus, in most colonies before the gold rush the general procedure was for the governments to subsidize the major religious sects, usually the Anglicans, Roman Catholics, Presbyterians, and Wesleyans, partly in order to assist these churches in their self-imposed task of providing schools. However, some dissenting sects and not a few members of all Protestant churches rejected, or at least gravely mistrusted, government aid because they feared the measure of state control which might accompany it. Naturally, rejection of state aid and support for the "voluntary principle" was strongest in South Australia. In 1851 the newly established Provincial Legislative Council, inspired by Richard Davies Hanson who had helped draft the Durham Report, ended all subsidies to churches and set up a Central Board of Education on which no minister of religion might serve. The Board's task was to administer a secular "national" system of schools, in which teachers might read from the Bible but might not give any kind of denominational or dogmatic religious instruction. Education in these South Australian "national" schools was not yet, however, either free or compulsory. Churches, naturally, remained free to maintain their own schools on the "voluntary" principle.

Meanwhile, Victoria and New South Wales established a dual system, maintaining a number of "national," undenominational schools, while at the same time continuing state aid to churches. The dual system proved increasingly costly and inefficient. Some districts had more schools than they could support, while others had too few or none at all. Moreover, those dissenting groups which refused, on voluntarist principles, to accept government aid tended to resent its acceptance by others, and there were many voluntarists even in the Church of England. While leaders of religious opinion wrangled, an increasing number of liberal-minded men pressed ever more strongly for a single, national system (within each colony) of "free, compulsory and secular" education which, they hoped, would at least succeed in teaching the "three R's" to all children irrespective of the wealth or religious beliefs of their parents. Among these people was a relatively small but influential group of radical secularists, men like the novelists "Rolf Boldrewood" and Marcus Clarke who, if not always convinced rationalists, were at least positive anticlericals. Many sincerely religious people also opposed sectarian control of education because they felt it tended to perpetuate, or even create, class and "national" divisions in the Australian community.

The last argument was held by some to apply with special force to the Roman Catholic schools, for in Australia the great majority of the Catholic priesthood and laity were Irish by descent and so were suspected by traditionalists of disaffection. At the same time, the Catholic religious body as a whole was almost solidly united in opposition to the introduction of a "national" system. In June 1879 the Catholic Archbishop of Sydney denounced secular schools in a pastoral letter, declaring that they were "seed-plots of future immorality, infidelity, and lawlessness, being calculated to debase the standards of human excellence, and to corrupt the political, social, and individual life of future citizens." While the controversy lasted, some secularist leaders at least matched the intemperance of this language. The same resolution of the conflict was reached in all the colonies, though at different times. State aid to church schools was withdrawn and national (i.e., colony-wide) systems of state-supported and -controlled education were set up. If these state schools were not at first entirely free, they soon became so—as well as secular, and compulsory in the sense that children who did not attend voluntary church schools were obliged by law to attend the state schools. The decisive acts were passed in Victoria in 1872, in South Australia and Queensland in 1875, and in New South Wales in 1880.

Yet both religious and secular prophets of woe did not see their fears, or hopes, fulfilled. Thenceforth, the great majority of all Australian children attended the state schools—and became on the whole more law-abiding than their progenitors had been. On the other hand, Roman Catholics, by prodigious efforts, established their own religious school system. Nearly all Catholic children have attended these schools ever since, and few observers believe that their existence has had a seriously divisive effect on the Australian community. Why American Catholics should, for the most part, have taken an opposite course by going along until quite recent times with the United States secular public school systems, when they were established at about the same period, is a question that has seldom been asked in Australia. It may be that Americans, with their vastly higher proportion of citizens and immigrants of non-British descent, attached much greater weight to the role of the public school as an assimilating, unifying agent.

Free Trade Versus Protection

To contemporaries, fiscal policy seemed to be a most important, as well as a most divisive, issue: and this is strange because the historian, even with the benefit of hindsight, cannot see that either free trade or protection conferred marked advantages on the colonies that adopted them. Yet in so far as politicians of the period divided on questions of fixed principle at all, they did so on fiscal policy. In the last two decades of the nineteenth century organized free trade and protectionist parties appeared in most of the legislatures. This development occurred even earlier in Victoria, which adopted increasingly high protective tariffs from 1866 onward. Tasmania and South Australia, though less enthusiastically, followed the Victorian lead, partly perforce, as their economies were largely dependent on Victoria's. New South Wales remained throughout the period resolutely wedded to free trade, while Queensland maintained an uneasy position of compromise.

It may be that the greater proportion of Americans in Victoria, the premier gold-mining colony, had some influence on the early growth of protectionist sentiment there. More important, certainly, was the business recession, accompanied by mounting unemployment in the towns, which set in after 1857 when the most easily won gold had been worked out. It is hard also to overestimate the importance of David Syme, a young Scots radical who came looking for gold but stayed to become proprietor of the Melbourne *Age*, then and still one of the most influential newspapers in the continent. It has been suggested, not altogether jestingly, that New South Wales stuck to free trade for no better reason than that its younger but more populous rival became protectionist. It is also true that the wool industry, which in Australia has never needed fiscal protection from any competitor, continued to occupy a more prominent position in the mother colony than in any of the others: and Henry Parkes, the most influential Sydney politician throughout the period, remained an inflexible free trader. Customhouses were established along the colonial borders, though population was so sparse that it was impossible to prevent smuggling. The opposed fiscal policies gave rise to much political rhetoric and to much jealousy, especially between New South Wales and Victoria; yet both prospered. Secondary industry increased in Victoria at a somewhat faster rate than it did in New South Wales, but the population of the latter colony grew more quickly. During the last decade of the century it resumed its place as the most populous of all the colonies. Yet after federation in 1901 it was protection which became the fixed policy of the Commonwealth.

Bourgeoisie and Bushrangers

We have seen that throughout this period of steady, if unspectacular, growth the leading role was played in the capital cities by liberal, middle-class people, most of whom were immigrants. The wage-earning majority of citizens took little active part, and relatively little interest, in politics, while the Australian-born minority of mature voters had little scope for giving political or other overt expression to the nationalist (as distinct from democratic) aspirations of which we saw inchoate signs before the gold rush. It may be that, to a small but significant extent, bushranging gave a symbolic form to these half-formed nationalist sentiments.

Visiting writers during the 1860's and 1870's were much impressed by the prevalence of bushranging. John Martineau called it "the peculiar institution" of the country, thereby consciously comparing it with slavery in the southern United States as an institution discreditable in itself, but one to which most of the citizens were strongly attached. Martineau was right, for bushranging was distinguished from similar lawlessness in the United States and elsewhere mainly by the extraordinarily widespread sympathy felt for the criminals. He was right too in remarking that the institution flourished principally in the mother colony which (with Tasmania) had the highest proportion of native-born citizens. Without at least the tacit support of the majority of bush-workers and free-selectors, the most accomplished scoundrels would have been captured in days or weeks. As it was, they commonly ranged at will for months or years, robbing for the most part from the rich who were most worth the trouble, and giving to the poor considerable quantities—at least of other people's rum. When arrested and taken for trial to the capital cities, they were often given heroes' welcomes by large crowds.

This widespread sympathy stemmed from convict days when emancipist-exclusionist enmity had run high; but there is evidence that it was also in part a symbolic and only half-conscious expression of lower class and nationalist resentment at the *de facto* exclusion of these elements from any considerable political and social influence on events during the period. The name of Ned Kelly, native-born and bush-bred son of an emancipist free-selector, and most colorful of the outlaws, is firmly entrenched in Australian language, literature, and art. "As game as Ned Kelly" is a household expression throughout the continent. In 1964 a huge traffic snarl in the center of Sydney was caused by a car bearing a Victorian number plate. Good temper all round was restored when a Sydney driver shouted at the embarrassed Victorian, "Where do you come from, mate—Glenrowan?" No frustrated driver had to be told the name of the Victorian town where Kelly was finally cornered and caught. As an opposing symbol we may take Sir Redmond Barry, free immigrant of respectable middle-class background and liberal views. Barry was first chancellor of the University of Melbourne where stonemasons had been working in 1856 when they struck for the eight-hour day. He was first president of the trustees of the Public Library of Victoria and of the Melbourne Mechanics' Institute, and from 1852 a judge of the Victorian Supreme Court. He was one of the worthiest citizens of his day and his statue stands before the main entrance to Melbourne's Public Library: yet few people even in Victoria notice it and fewer now remember his name, though many pilgrims visit the nearby Exhibition Building to see Ned Kelly's armor.

In November 1880 Barry closed the bushranger's trial by pronouncing the words, "Edward Kelly, I hereby sentence you to death by hanging. May the Lord have mercy on your soul." In a clear, level voice the outlaw replied, "Yes, I will meet you there!" As it happened, Barry died about a fortnight later; but the most celebrated trial in Australian history may have had some more general historic significance, at least of an allegorical sort. During the following thirty years or so the two opposing, yet interpenetrating, streams of influence symbolized by the two men did meet; and they coalesced to a remarkable degree, though in ways which would on the whole have pleased Sir Redmond more than Ned. We shall outline this process in the following chapter.

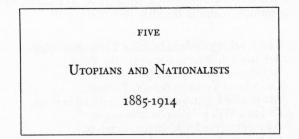

Many Australians look back on the 1890's in somewhat the same way as Americans remember their Revolutionary Age. As Vance Palmer wrote in his *Legend of the Nineties* (Melbourne, 1954, p. 9):

> There has grown up a legend of the Australian nineties as a period of intense artistic and political activity, in which the genius of this young country had a brief and brilliant first flowering. Something new, it is claimed, emerged into the light. A scattered people, with origins in all corners of the British Islands and in Europe, had a sudden vision of themselves as a nation, with a character of their own and a historic role to play, and this vision set fruitful creative forces in motion.

Middle-Class Nationalism

As Palmer goes on to say, this vision "had a close connection with historical reality." In the thirty years or so between about 1885 and the outbreak of the First World War Australians became conscious, not to say self-conscious, of their nationhood, gave this sentiment formal political expression by establishing the federal government, and hammered out broadly accepted national policies which have largely determined the course of later developments. After a hundred years much of what the Currency Lads had felt, and the bushrangers had symbolized, was accepted by most middle-class Australians— though largely in their own terms—as part of the image of the new nation. Yet since many men also felt that there was, in the brief national past, insufficient on which to build a proud tradition, the awakening patriotic sentiment was strongly colored by a strand of utopian idealism which looked to the future. Unhampered by the inherited quarrels and entrenched injustices of older countries, Australia should become the exemplar of the just society of the common man—the white Australian common man, of course. This mood was captured exactly by a contemporary poet, Bernard O'Dowd, a native-born son of a trooper in the Victorian Gold Escort who engaged in a long and friendly correspondence with Walt Whitman. O'Dowd's well-known sonnet *Australia* begins:

> Last sea-thing dredged by sailor Time from Space,
> Are you a drift Sargasso, where the West
> In halcyon calm rebuilds her fatal nest?
> Or Delos of a coming Sun-God's race?
> Are you for Light, and trimmed, with oil in place,
> Or but a Will o' Wisp on marshy quest?
> A new demesne for Mammon to infest?
> Or lurks millennial Eden 'neath your face?

The importance of this utopian theme has often been exaggerated by later writers. So has the extent of the influence on events exercised by radicals and visionaries in the working-class or "Labor" movement. Self-interest, and economic and political horse-trading, played as big a part in the Australian Nineties as they customarily do in human affairs. Yet historians generally agree that this is the crucial period for an understanding of modern Australia, especially for an understanding of whatever is distinctive about the tone and texture of Australian life.

In the last chapter we saw that the great influx of mid-century gold-rush immigrants accelerated the growth of democratic institutions, while at the same time it delayed the growth of Australian nationalism—at any rate among the more cultivated and articulate sections of society. We must now notice that, from about 1860 onward, immigration could be more properly likened to a steady if substantial trickle than to a flood. The result was that while the gold-rush immigrants were being gradually but thoroughly acclimatized, the proportion of native-born people in the country as a whole rose far above the 43 per cent it had reached in New South Wales in 1851. White natives comprised 60 per cent of the continent's total population in 1871, 75 per cent in 1891, and 82 per cent in 1901. This growing preponderance of the native-born was probably the greatest single underlying cause of the growth of national sentiment toward the end of the century: for while immigrants naturally tended to feel more British than Australian patriotic sentiment, the natives had from the earliest days tended to regard themselves—intercolonial rivalries notwithstanding—as Australians first and only in certain contexts as Victorians, Queenslanders, and so forth. At no time did regional differences develop to anything like the extent that they did in the United States and Canada; this was partly because of the national and cultural homogeneity of practically all of the colonists, and partly because the predominantly pastoral and mining economy of nineteenth century Australia promoted much more movement and mixing of the colonial populations than did the predominantly agricultural North American economy.

It should be noted too that mining, though for base metals rather than gold, continued to be of fundamental importance. In 1883 one of the richest silver-lead-zinc fields in the world was discovered at Broken Hill, and only slightly less rich lodes, which included copper and tin ores, were found in the Mount Lyell region of Tasmania. There were few spectacular rushes connected with these and other discoveries, but profits from investment in the mining industry played a major part in Australian capital formation during the period surveyed in this chapter. Despite the great depression of the early 1890's, this capital aided in the modest though steady growth of secondary industry which had begun in the golden decade. Especially important was the Broken Hill Proprietary Company itself. From silver-lead-zinc mining in one state it expanded into other fields of enterprise and into other states. Rich iron ores were mined in South Australia and carried to the Newcastle coalfields, north of Sydney, there to lay the foundations of Australian heavy industry, while coal was carried back to South Australia to process some of the Broken Hill ores.

Perhaps the next most important force in the foundation of Australian secondary industry was the Colonial Sugar Refining Company, formed in 1855. Beginning with processing the sugar crop in Queensland and northern New South Wales coastal districts, the C. S. R., like the B. H. P., later moved into shipping—and acquired extensive interests in Fiji and New Zealand. With other new companies these two colonial giants laid in this period secure foundations on which Australian heavy industry and commerce built rapidly later, especially after World War Two.

By the end of the century, most middle-class Australians had begun to feel as much at home in the no-longer strange continent as working people had long felt, though often not in quite the same way. Well-to-do people, educated still almost exclusively in English literature, history, and culture, tended to think in the spirit of W. C. Wentworth's 1817 poem[1] of "a new Britannia in another world" rather than to accept, as the masses did without much conscious thought, the fact of Australia's own developing identity. Still, most Australians no longer thought of themselves as Britons living in temporary exile. It was time therefore to think about what they *were*. Moreover, at the practical tasks of pioneering, native-born people and experienced

[1] See p. 38.

old colonists had long been preferred by employers. In white-collar and professional occupations this was by no means the case. It was still assumed that the most important and well-paid positions in education, the church, and the professions, and even to a considerable extent in business, could usually be filled adequately only by British immigrants. Many were increasingly irked by this attitude in high places. Sir Samuel Griffith, scholarly premier of Queensland and one of the chief advocates of federal union, spoke for almost all his countrymen, irrespective of wealth, educational attainments, politics, or religion, when he said at the Federal Convention of 1891:

> I am tired of being called a Colonist. The term is used no doubt at the other end of the world without the slightest intention of using a disparaging expression, but unconsciously as a term of disparagement. The colonist is really regarded by the usage of the term as a person who is in some respects inferior, who does not enjoy the same advantages and is not quite entitled to the same privileges as other members of the Empire.

The patronizing attitude to which Griffith referred continued for long afterward to be voiced by eminent British sojourners in Australia and, by reaction, to accentuate the growing national sentiment. That it was often only unconsciously disparaging naturally rendered it more obnoxious, or ridiculous, to the "colonists." In 1901, for instance, Earl Beauchamp came out to govern, briefly, New South Wales. On landing he made a well-meaning speech in which, quoting Rudyard Kipling, he spoke of Australia's having turned her "birth-stains" to good. For years afterward the popular Sydney *Bulletin* filled occasional spaces at the foot of a column with a pseudo-advertisement: "For birth-stains, try Beauchamp's Pills!"—Beecham's Pills being one of the most widely advertised patent medicines of the period.

Irish-Australian Nationalism

None, naturally, reacted more strongly to English condescension than the Irish-Australians, who comprised about 20 per cent of the population. In convict times Irishmen and people of Irish descent had numbered about 30 per cent. From the beginning they had tended to acclimatize themselves more readily and completely than other immigrants: first because they were Irish, and second because a grossly disproportionate number of them were to be found among the unskilled, wage-earning section of the community. If, as many English and Scottish immigrants felt in the last century, Australian national sentiment savored rather of "disloyalty" to the Old Country, Irish immigrants naturally embraced it the more readily for that very reason. And working people generally, because they were on the average less well educated and less able to keep up cultural or other connections with Great Britain, inevitably took on the color of their surroundings more rapidly than was usual among the well-to-do. Possibly the Vatican was not unmindful of these factors when it chose bishops for the Australian colonies. At any rate, until the 1870's few Catholic prelates came from Ireland whence had sprung the vast majority of their flocks. Much more typical in the early period was R. W. B. Vaughan, Archbishop of Sydney from 1877 to 1883, an aristocratic Englishman one of whose ancestors had distinguished himself at the Battle of Agincourt. Among the mid-century immigrants there was a higher proportion of educated, middle-class Irishmen, both Protestant and Catholic, like Peter Lalor of Eureka fame or Charles Gavan Duffy, already well known when he emigrated for his leadership in the Irish home rule movement. It was probably no accident that Gavan Duffy, for a time premier of Victoria, also took a leading part in the early (and premature) federation movement.

In 1884 another and very remarkable Irishman came to Australia. Francis Patrick Moran, the new Catholic Archbishop of Sydney, announced on landing at Port Jackson, "On this day I become an Australian, and I am determined to live as an Australian for Australia." The contrast between this and the customary Earl Beauchamp type of pronunciamento made by newly arrived dignitaries was not lost on the inhabitants. Moran became the first Australian cardinal and worked prodigiously until his death in 1911. In addition to performing his purely pastoral duties and building the Catholic school system, he gave great encouragement to the emerging Labor Party[2] and played an active, possibly a decisive, part in nurturing pro-federation sentiment in New South Wales—the colony which was most reluctant to join in creating the new nation. His speeches and actions alike suggest that he foresaw, before many of its own members did, the rise of the Labor Party to a position of decisive political importance; that he realized that most Australian Catholics would, for economic reasons in any case, be attracted to it; and that, influenced by the ideals of social justice propounded in the 1891 Papal Encyclical De Rerum Novarum, he sought to strengthen the Labor movement no less than to ensure that it would be moderate, reformist, and nonrevolutionary in both its methods and aims. At the same time, he campaigned actively, far too actively some thought, for federation, even though Labor was for the most part officially opposed to federation, which

[2] For details of the relationship between the Catholic Church and the Labor Party, see J. F. Mason, Catholics and the Labor Movement in New South Wales 1890-1960 (Univ. New England, Litt B. thesis, 1963).

it suspected as a conservative device for distracting attention from social ills. Sir Henry Parkes, until his death the most prominent New South Wales federalist, had also been the father in that colony of free, compulsory, and secular education. As such, he tended to be regarded by Catholics as their chief political enemy. Yet Parkes said of Moran in a parliamentary speech of 1895:

> There is another person, who is an entire stranger to me, and, I should think, a gentleman who has no very high opinion of me, whose services I should acknowledge. Of all the voices on this question, no voice has been more distinct, more full of a worthy foreshadowing of the question's greatness and more fraught with a clear prescience of what is likely to come as a result of Federation, than the voice of this eminent prelate.

Thus for the first time the mass of the Australian people, including those of Irish descent, came to play an active role in shaping political and national life. Since they had long taken their basic Australianness for granted, it is not surprising that the period should have seen such an upsurge of nationalist sentiment—of which political federation was only one, and perhaps not the most fundamental, aspect.

Nationalism and the Arts

The new mood was manifested most dramatically in the arts. By the 1890's public education systems had made most people literate. A racy folk literature which clothed the once-strange environment with indigenous songs, tales, and figures of speech had long circulated orally among working people, particularly in the bush. Now a man who might once have helped improvise a new ballad was more likely to write it down and send it to a magazine for publication. More importantly journalists, poets, and other "accredited" literary men began to see Australian life directly with their own eyes rather than through the inherited spectacles of English literary and social conventions. Previously most Australian writing aspiring to the status of literature had been done primarily with a cultivated English audience in mind—even when the writer happened to be an Australian by birth; and of course some creative writers like Christopher Brennan continued at this period, and have continued since, to be little affected by the nationalist temper. There is nothing either odd or unhealthy about this. After all, English is the leading world language, and Henry James and T. S. Eliot remind us that even some American literary men of the first rank have continued to feel more at home in England than in their own country. But during and since the last decade of the last century most Australian literature has been written primarily about Australian life and for an Australian audience. Less emphatically, the same can be said of the visual arts. In the same period men like Tom Roberts, Arthur Streeton, Frederick McCubbin, and Charles Conder established a distinctively Australian tradition of painting which, like the new literature, tended to emphasize outback life because it was felt to be more characteristically Australian than life in the cities. These painters are often spoken of as belonging to the Heidelberg School. The name comes from a village on the outskirts of Melbourne where some of them established a camp and worked together.

In literature the great names were A. B. ("Banjo") Paterson (1864-1941), Henry Lawson (1867-1922), and Joseph Furphy ("Tom Collins") (1843-1912), but many lesser men like Victor Daley, Bernard O'Dowd, Francis Adams, Roderick Quinn, and C. J. Dennis produced significant work in the same genre. At its worst their writing was slipshod and "near enough" in execution and brash and bumptious in manner, being far too self-consciously concerned with "Australianism." Establishd and tradition-minded critics were quick to emphasize these weaknesses. In the preface to his great novel, first published in 1903, Furphy unrepentantly rejoined that his work was "in temper democratic, bias offensively Australian," and his title *Such Is Life* is held to have been Ned Kelly's last utterance from the gallows. At its best the new writing was original, idiomatic, vigorous, and absolutely true to the Australian experience. As suggested by Furphy's remark, it was concerned equally with nationalism and with democratic egalitarianism. Indeed to many if not most contemporaries, nationalism and leveling, democratic ideas seemed merely different aspects of a single ideal, summed up in its most romantically exaggerated form by the *Bulletin* in an editorial of 2 July 1887:

> By the term Australian we mean not those who have been merely born in Australia. All white men who come to these shores—with a clean record—and who leave behind them the memory of the class-distinctions and the religious differences of the old world; all men who place the happiness, the prosperity, the advancement of their adopted country before the interests of Imperialism, are Australian. . . . In this regard all men . . . who leave their fatherland because they cannot swallow the worm-eaten lie of the divine right of kings to murder peasants, are Australians by instinct—Australian and Republican are synonymous.

The *Bulletin* was a weekly journal first published in Sydney in 1880. Under the editorial guidance of J. F. Archibald, its policy was strongly nationalist, radical, and republican. After the achievement of federation in 1901 republicanism was quietly dropped from its program, and it became less radical and less "anti-Imperialist" or anti-British with the years, but it did not take on its later conservative coloring until about the time of the First World War.[3] The early *Bulletin* was immensely popular and far more influential than any Australian journal before or since. After its first few years it circulated widely in all the colonies, not just in New South Wales. In keeping with the widespread feeling that truly or "typically" Australian values were to be found in bush life, the paper gave disproportionate space to outback news, views, and themes. It came to be known as "the bushman's Bible"; it is said that the diggers on the Western Australian goldfields declared a holiday when copies reached them, but in fact it was read in almost every barber shop in the cities as well as in those of the country towns. Its success sprang partly from Archibald's policy of encouraging reader participation. Every issue contained many short, pungent paragraphs sent in by readers; and in one of these readers, A. G. Stephens, whom Archibald made the paper's literary editor, the *Bulletin* found the first Australian literary critic of stature. Almost every Australian writer of the period found a congenial forum in its columns. Yet literature, after all, reflected the national mood quite as much as it created it. The same may be said of politics. What were the significant changes in this sphere?

The "New Unionism"

Most important and far-reaching in its effects was the movement of the working class into active participation in political life. We have seen that wage earners took little direct part in politics before this time; but by about 1890 the education acts, together with liberal measures such as payment of members of Parliament, had done much to make the direct representation of wage earners in the legislatures at least possible. At the same time a new kind of industrial trade unionism sprang up, not only in Australia of course, but in Western Europe and North America. We remember that small, exclusive craft-unions had won the eight-hour day for some skilled tradesmen in the large Australian cities as early as 1856; but the new industrial unions sought to embrace all workers, including semiskilled men and even unskilled laborers. They were more or less strongly influenced by European and American radical ideas. In fact the two "socialist" tracts most influential in Australia at the period were both American

[3] For changes in the *Bulletin*'s political policies see Peter Cady, *The Political Policy of the Sydney "Bulletin" 1890-1901* (Univ. New England, B.A. thesis, 1962) and N. D. Green, *The "Bulletin"—Political Changes, 1900-1918* (Univ. New England, B.A. thesis, 1963).

works—Henry George's *Progress and Poverty,* and Edward Bellamy's
Looking Backward. William Lane, the most influential Labor journalist in Australia, reprinted *Looking Backward* in serial form in the
Brisbane *Worker.* However this is to anticipate a little. In the United
States, Canada, Great Britain, and elsewhere the new unionism was
based primarily on organizations of miners and transport workers.
In Australia also these groups were important, but perhaps less so
on balance than the pastoral workers. Rural laborers are traditionally
conservative and slow to join trade unions, but in Australia most
bushmen worked on large pastoral holdings where the impersonal
relation between employer and employee was more like that in a
large urban factory than in a small farm or business. William Guthrie
Spence, leading union organizer of the period and later a Labor member of the federal Parliament, described the appeal of the new unionism to the bush-workers thus:

> Unionism came to the Australian bushman as a religion. . . . It had
> in it that feeling of mateship which he understood already, and which
> always characterised the action of one "white man" to another. Union-
> ism extended the idea, so a man's character was gauged by whether he
> stood true to Union rules or "scabbed" it on his fellows. . . . The
> lowest form of reproach is to call a man a "scab." . . . At many a
> country ball the girls have refused to dance with them, the barmaids
> have refused them a drink, and the waitresses a meal.

The Amalgamated Shearers' Union, founded in 1886, organized
bush-workers in New South Wales, Victoria, and South Australia.
The Queensland Shearers' Union, begun in the same year, worked
smoothly with the A. S. U. until both organizations merged under
Spence's leadership in the Australian Workers' Union, still the most
powerful, though no longer the most militant, trade union in Australia. The new unions did not condone violence, and they preferred
negotiation to strikes. Nevertheless, it was a time of falling wool
prices, and there were more strikes in the pastoral industry between
1886 and 1889 than in all other Australian industries put together.
At first the unions were generally successful in maintaining working
conditions at the existing level, and they even won some concessions
from employers. Trade unionism in Australia was stronger than in
any other country at the time. The high degree of optimism and
idealism among union members was dramatically shown when the
London dock-workers were on strike in 1889. Not without some feeling of condescension to the "backward" English workers, Australian
sympathizers contributed £30,000—say $400,000 in terms of purchas-
ing power in the mid-1960's—to the London strike fund. The gift

had a decisive effect on the strike's success.[4] In the following year of crisis when Australian strikers needed help, British sympathizers contributed £4,060. The onset of the great depression of 1890-1894 had a strong catalytic effect on the developing Labor movement. It also stimulated nationalist sentiment and—what was not always quite the same thing—sentiment in favor of a federal union of the colonies.

The Depression of the Nineties

The long-continued expansion of the Seventies and Eighties had been based mainly on over-optimistic borrowing, both governmental and private, from British investors. In "Marvellous Melbourne" speculation was such that real estate prices of some central city blocks soared to levels higher than any reached again for about fifty years. As wool, wheat, and base metal prices continued to fall, foreclosures and bankruptcies snowballed into a financial panic. In 1893 most banks in Australia suspended payment and were laboriously reconstructed, while many failed completely. All the colonies were hard hit except Western Australia, where rich gold discoveries at the same period gave that previously backward part of the continent its first real boom. Scores of thousands of men from the eastern colonies—unemployed laborers, clerks, and even redundant bank managers—sailed to the west to try their luck, and most of them stayed. The young Herbert Hoover was one of the comparatively few overseas fortune-seekers to join the Western Australian gold rush. The land of "sand, sin, sorrow and sore eyes" began to be called instead the "Golden West." That the depression was more severe in Victoria than in New South Wales was partly due to the cool and astute handling of the banking crisis in the latter colony by its premier, Sir George Dibbs, who was moved to write in 1894: "It is not, indeed, too much to say that the Banking panic here largely arose through British withdrawals, and was intensified by fears that British depositors would secure their money first."[5] Few citizens had Dibbs's knowledge of the money market, but many found their nationalist aspirations strengthened by the belief that the machinations of British financiers had significantly helped to cause all the unemployment and distress. Before the depression reached its nadir, however, what Australians still often call "the great strikes" of the Nineties had begun.

[4] Henry Pelling, *History of British Trade Unionism* (Harmondsworth, 1963), pp. 99-100.

[5] C. M. H. Clark, *Select Documents in Australian History 1851-1900* (Sydney, 1955), p. 313.

"The Great Strikes"

The first Inter-colonial Trade Union Congress was held in 1879, and the second in 1884. Thereafter, congresses met annually or bi-ennially and carried resolutions which became more militant in tone and more implicitly "political" in nature as the new industrial unions gathered strength. The Congress of 1888, which met in Brisbane, planned a nationwide trade union organization with a central leader-ship to coordinate both industrial and political policies. At the same time, as we have seen, the shearers were remarkably successful at resisting the understandable attempts of pastoralists to pass on the effect of falling wool prices by cutting the standard wage of £1 per hundred sheep shorn. Naturally trade union militancy and combina-tion were met by a reaction among employers, who also began to combine in such organizations as the Pastoralists' Union with its own Federal Council. In such ways federation was becoming a fact of Australian life long before it became a fact of Australian politics. Some trade-union leaders even urged the formation of employers' associations so as to facilitate bargaining for minimum wages, as they hoped, by workers in every industry in the country; and in 1890 a Queensland wharf-laborers' strike helped force on the squatters an agreement to employ none but union labor in their shearing sheds. Such successes invited emulation, and the radical movement's force was shown by the extraordinary fact that the maritime strike, which precipitated the trial of strength between Capital and Labor, was triggered not by the demands of manual workers but by the action of ships' *officers*. Having formed a trade union of their own, the marine officers affiliated with the Melbourne Trades Hall Council. It was too much for the shipowners. They refused even to discuss the officers' other claims until they withdrew their affiliation and stopped behaving like common workmen. In August 1890 the officers walked off the ships in defense, as they saw it, of their right to form a trade union and associate with others for the common good, or to refuse, in pursuit of the same ends, to associate with nonunionists. The employers, of course, saw the great principle involved equally clearly, but from an opposite point of view. They fought, as they saw it, for freedom of contract—for their right to employ whomsoever they chose at mutually agreed rates of payment and without union inter-ference. Within hours of the officers' action the employers had advertised for nonunion wharf laborers, and within a month tens of thousands of unionists—seamen, waterside workers, miners, pastoral workers, and others—were on strike. The marine officers' dispute was almost lost to sight in this head-on clash of principle between Capital and Labor.

The "great maritime strike" was defeated over the course of the next month or so, but the struggle was renewed again and again, especially by the bush-workers, until 1894. The "rebel" Southern Cross flag of Eureka Stockade was raised over some of the strikers' camps in Queensland, and hotheads on both sides talked at times of civil war: but though brawls and bad words were common enough and arson occurred, there seems to have been no loss of life. In preserving "law and order" the colonial governments collaborated with employers' organizations while the press almost unanimously denounced those of the employees. Twelve trade-union leaders were arrested and charged under an act of George IV, which had been repealed in Great Britain but not in the colony of Queensland. Acquitted by a jury, they were re-arrested, charged with conspiracy, and sentenced to three years' imprisonment. By the end of 1894 "freedom of contract" had been temporarily established, and the trade-union movement, employers felt, had been taught a lesson— not so devastatingly, however, as to prevent its regaining by the end of the century its former numerical and organizational strength, if not quite its former militancy. Under the leadership of William Lane, a few hundred idealists sailed away to South America to found, in the wilds of Paraguay, a socialist community to be known as New Australia; but the defeat of the strikes caused more practical Labor leaders to turn more decidedly toward parliamentary action. In their view all the colonial governments, whether Free Trade or Protectionist in complexion, had taken sides with the employers against the employees; while the clergy, with a handful of notable exceptions, had left the people of Australia to "grope amidst the gloom of sacerdotal clap-trap." Easily the most notable exception had been Cardinal Moran, for whom a strike procession had given three cheers as the men marched past St. Mary's Cathedral in Sydney.

Rise of the Labor Party

Yet the defeat of the strikes did not much more than accelerate the Labor movement's entry into the political field. In New South Wales, for instance, thirty-six Labor Party members who held the balance of power in the Legislative Assembly had been elected to Parliament in 1891, and by 1893 a similar situation existed in Queensland. In the southern colonies, partly because more liberal legislation had already been enacted there by radical middle-class politicians, Labor parties gained influence—and internal cohesion—more slowly, but essentially the same changes took place. Oddly enough, in view of the stress Labor from the first placed on party organization and discipline, the six colonial (after 1901, state) Labor parties did not formally set up a nationwide organization until 1915—years after the party had grown quite accustomed to occupying the treasury benches in the national Parliament. From the time when Labor members were first elected, the party programs stressed practical reformist measures rather than any kind of general, doctrinaire socialist plans for reconstructing society. Until 1909 Labor usually held the balance of power in the various parliaments and openly offered "support in return for concessions" to rival parties which wished to form governments. Thus, even before federation, most colonial governments with Labor support—perhaps pressure would be a more appropriate word—enacted a good deal of social legislation which sought both to make the economy work more effectively and to protect less fortunate citizens from its untrammeled operations. Much of this legislation was accepted by conservatives as well as liberals—at least partly because of the great strikes. Most men, wishing to avoid any further such experience, were readier than they had earlier been to accept, even to applaud, some forms of state interference in industry. Thus most colonies during the Nineties set up some kind of legal machinery for arbitrating disputes between employers and employees. Minimum working conditions and maximum hours of labor were laid down in a number of factory and mining acts, while early closing acts protected shop assistants from what was felt to be too incessant work. Under closer settlement acts governments repurchased land from pastoralists or land companies, subdivided it, and sold it back on easy terms to small farmers to whom they lent money until they were able to stand on their own feet. Such legislation was considerably more successful in establishing small men on the land than the selection acts of the previous thirty years had been. Most colonies, largely under Henry George's influence, introduced land taxes—both to raise revenue and, some hoped, to help break up the large pastoral estates. Old age pension schemes were also established in the two largest colonies by the end of the century.

It must not be thought that all these reforms were simply and solely the result of Labor pressure. Many middle-class politicians of the traditionally established Free Trade and Protectionist parties held genuinely "progressive" views and, on some measures, needed no pushing from their allies. Moreover, on the matter of setting up arbitration courts, for example, Labor was by no means solidly enthusiastic. Its view of the state's role in the great strike struggles suggested to some, rather, that state arbitration might prove another employers' device for coercing the wage earners. Still, Labor's influence in bringing about this plethora of social legislation was unquestionably considerable.

Its influence on the organizational forms of Australian politics was possibly greater and certainly easier to demonstrate. We have seen that during the first thirty years or so of responsible government organized parties hardly existed, and that consequently politicians were even freer than they are today in the United States to vote as conscience, or interest, directed them. On the whole, politicians had been much more impressed with the merits of this situation than had the electors. So the founders of the Labor Party in the various colonies sought for some way of binding their parliamentary representatives to the policies of those whose votes were to send them to the seats of the mighty. Thus was evolved the "pledge" and the "caucus." Every Labor member pledged himself to carry out the party program, as determined primarily by the extra-parliamentary organizations of the party, and to this end he promised to cast his vote on every question as decided beforehand by a caucus, or private meeting, of Labor members of parliament. Newspaper editors and traditionalists of all hues thundered at what they saw as the wickedness of these arrangements. Their most plausible argument was that Labor procedures, by predetermining outside parliament the party's vote, made a mere mockery of the parliamentary process of debate and decision. Labor members were denounced as "mere delegates" or mechanical puppets who had sold their own souls, it was implied, to the Devils in charge of the Trades and Labor Councils. Nevertheless, the Free Trade and Protectionist parties or groupings, if only in self-defense, were compelled by Labor's example to tighten party discipline and strengthen their own organizations in other ways. An important side effect of this process was to help make Australian political life cleaner on the whole in the twentieth century than it had been in the nineteenth. Stricter party discipline both reduced the area for devious maneuver available to individual members and made them more responsible to their electors—or at least more responsible to the fixed principles for which the electors now knew the fixed parties claimed to stand. Yet this alignment of parties with principles took place only gradually. Throughout the 1890's in most colonies Labor avoided commitment in principle to either free trade or protection, while no party as such stood unequivocally for federation.

Nationalism and Federation

It is clear that nationalist sentiment was increasing in all sections of the community, but the keenest nationalists did not always see federal union as the necessary, or even desirable, way of giving effect to their aspirations. The *Bulletin*, for instance, preached nationalism more fervently than any other journal, but was anti-federalist till the last three or four years of the century. Because some conservative opinion supported Australian federation, the *Bulletin* for long suspected it as a stalking-horse for the bringing about of Imperial federation. The latter was a *fin-de-siècle* scheme, agitated for but never very clearly defined by some British politicians and publicists, for forming some sort of federal Imperial government to which the self-governing colonies at least should send representatives. The plan roused little enthusiasm in Australia even among conservatives, certainly no more and perhaps less than did the republican visions of some radicals and liberals: but its effect on the federal movement exemplifies the complex manner in which the federation issue was enmeshed with so many others. Yet it is clear that the rising tide of nationalist sentiment did increasingly spill over into the federal movement, and that to a considerable extent it forced the hands of some important politicians like George Houston ("Yes-No") Reid, Free Trade premier of New South Wales from 1894 to 1898. It is less clear, but probably equally true, that federation sentiment was strongest among working-class and middle-of-the-road citizens and weakest among conservatives. Yet this could not be easily deduced from the behavior of politicians. Generally speaking, Labor's political leaders actively opposed, or at best were lukewarm toward, federation. Conservatives, whether Free Trade or Protectionist in complexion, were divided. Overwhelmingly the lead came from liberal middle-class politicians like Alfred Deakin of Victoria, Sir Henry Parkes of New South Wales, and Charles Cameron Kingston of South Australia.

Such men and their supporters were inspired by a sincere and often deeply felt patriotism, but they were also highly practical politicians who seldom lost sight of more mundane matters. They thought, rightly, that federation would pay. Tasmania, for instance, with its small area and largely rural population, depended heavily upon its exports of agricultural produce to the mainland colonies. One federal propagandist in the "Apple Isle" found the following speech enormously effective:

> Gentlemen, if you vote for the Bill you will found a great and glorious nation under the bright Southern Cross, and meat will be cheaper; and you will live to see the Australian race dominate the Southern seas, and you will have a market for both potatoes and apples; and your sons shall reap the grand heritage of nationhood, and if Sir William Lyne does come back to power in Sydney he can never do you one pennyworth of harm.[6]

[6] B. R. Wise, *The Making of the Australian Commonwealth 1889-1900* (London, 1913), p. 356.

Lyne was the Protectionist leader in New South Wales who, it was feared, might ruin Tasmania by introducing tariffs to protect the mother colony's agriculture against Tasmanian competition.

There is space in this book barely to mention some of the major arguments of the federationists and the series of convocations and referenda by which union was brought about. The story has been well told in many standard histories. As the last British soldier had left Australia in 1870, the need for a unified system of national defense was much canvassed. Many men, especially in border districts like the Riverina, were increasingly irked by intercolonial customs barriers; and many merchants, especially in Victoria where manufacturing industry was strongest, looked to the advantages of a continentwide market. Almost everyone agreed that a national government could best deal with questions of immigration and relations with foreign powers, especially with those like Germany and France which had interests in the Pacific. But one underlying factor of prime importance has not always been given the attention it merits: namely, the newly acquired physical propinquity of the separate colonies. Founded separately, and to a considerable extent settled separately from distant Britain, each colony had for long been a distinct community, centered on its coastal capital and separated from each of its neighbors by hundreds of miles of virgin wilderness. But the gold discoveries of the Fifties and the slow but steady spread of agricultural settlement thereafter, brought people, townships, roads, and finally telegraphs and railways, to the bush. By 1872 all towns of any size on the continent were in telegraphic communication with each other and with Great Britain, and by 1888 the four major colonial capitals—Melbourne, Sydney, Brisbane, and Adelaide—were joined by rail. Except for Western Australia, the separate colonies had already become one in a geographical sense, and Western Australia secured the promise of a railway link from the federal government as a condition of its joining. Even so, the West would probably not have joined until later if it had not been for the overwhelming pro-federation vote on her goldfields of the "t'other-siders" from the eastern colonies. But there had never been any really significant racial, linguistic, cultural, or even economic differences between the people of the various Australian colonies, as there had been in the United States and Canada. Now that settlement had spread through the bush until the colonies fused geographically it was natural, if not quite inevitable, that they should join to make one nation in the formal political sense, as they had long done informally in the broadest cultural sense. Indeed, it is not too much to suggest that, just because of this implicitly existing natural unity, the Commonwealth's founding fathers felt they could afford to follow the American precedent of leaving all residual powers to the states; while Canada's confederationists, in 1867 at the end of the American Civil War, were so conscious of French-speaking Quebec and other divisive regional differences that they felt constrained to reserve all residual powers for the central government.

Ever since 1847 some politicians in Britain and Australia had made sporadic federation proposals. All were abortive, primarily because they were premature in the above sense. The beginning of the final successful movement dates from a speech made in 1889 by Sir Henry Parkes in which, as an eyewitness reported: "for the first time the voice of an authoritative statesman gave soul and utterance to the aspirations of a people. It was truly remarkable and not without a touch of sublimity." Nor was it accidental that the ancient political warrior, more sensitive than any of his competitors to the ground swell of public opinion, gave tongue to his "clarion call" at Tenterfield, a large New South Wales country town on the newly completed railway joining the Queensland system at the border only a dozen or two miles to the north. From this time onward federation became an increasingly real issue. Yet the first round of conferences and conventions ended abortively in 1891, largely because the whole question was still being dealt with at an intergovernment level. After this check, bands of devoted federalists, many of them young, liberal-minded middle-class people like Dr. John Quick, set about rousing and articulating public opinion so that politicians would be compelled to respond effectively to it. Voluntary, nonparty political bodies, such as the Australian Natives' Association and the Federal League, played a leading part. The second round of convention meetings in 1897-1898 succeeded largely because of the strong popular movement which by then inspired the delegates and in spite of the very real difficulties of hammering out a workable and acceptable constitution.

Perhaps the most intractable problem was that of somehow reconciling responsible government in the British sense, i.e., responsibility of the prime minister and his cabinet to the popularly elected lower house, with the necessary federal principle of equality of rights for the constituent states. If the states' House or Senate were given equal powers with the House of Representatives elected on a population basis, how could the majority be said to rule, since more than two-thirds of the Australian people lived in the two prospective states of New South Wales and Victoria? On the other hand, if the two houses were not given equal powers, how could it be claimed that the six states, which were of course to be equally represented only in the

Senate, would be upon a footing of equality? Naturally, the constitutions of the United States and Canada were closely studied by some convention delegates, and freely argued about by all. The above difficulty was solved by a series of compromises, and the constitution finally recommended to the people owed a great deal to that of the United States. Indeed, in many respects the Australian constitution is modeled directly upon that of America. The Commonwealth's High Court, for example, like the American Supreme Court, is not only a tribunal to which litigants may appeal from the state supreme courts, but it also plays a very important and independent role in government through its power of interpreting the federal constitution.

The draft constitution was confirmed by popular referenda and then enacted as a statute by the British Parliament in London. The birth of the new nation was formally proclaimed on the first day of the new century, 1 January 1901. Its flag appropriately symbolized the marriage which had been consummated between traditional British values and the new indigenous values springing from a century's struggle with the harsh, but no longer strange, continent. The Union Jack and a large white star symbolizing the unity of the six states are balanced by the stars of the Southern Cross first flown at Eureka Stockade. It was no shot-gun wedding, but a genuine love match at which Lord Hopetoun, as the Queen's representative and new governor-general, served as the officiating clergyman. Hopetoun was also a daring horseman who, during his stay in Melbourne, made friends and exchanged autographed photographs with "Chummy" Fleming, secretary of the city's unemployed and for long Victoria's most dedicated, if not its only, anarchist.

Basic Commonwealth Legislation

The breadth of the existing consensus is indicated by the impressive legislative achievements of the first Commonwealth parliaments. It is hardly too much to say that they fixed the broad lines of development along which Australian society has moved ever since: and this despite the fact that until 1909 three parties, none of which ever had a clear majority by itself, contended for power. For these nine years each of the Free Trade, Protectionist, and Labor parties continued to win roughly a third of the seats—give or take a few— in the federal Parliament; though Labor's share continued to increase at the expense of the two middle-class groups. Though there were liberal Free Traders and conservative Protectionists, the Free Trade Party was, generally speaking, farthest to the right. It drew much support from chambers of commerce, importing agencies, and the strong pastoral interest. The Protectionists naturally enjoyed the support of manufacturers and other business interests struggling to build up local secondary industries against overseas competitors; and partly for this reason they attracted the votes of many keen nationalists. The party had a strong liberal wing and properly enough came to be known as the Liberal-Protectionist, or often simply the Liberal Party. The Labor Party of course claimed to stand for the interests of trade unionists and wage earners in general, and it retained as good a claim as the Protectionists to be the party of Australian nationalism; but the faint note of doctrinaire socialism became even fainter as its parliamentary members began to savor the delights of place and to be chastened by the responsibilities of power. Still, Labor usually sought to carry liberal reforms further and faster than even the most radical of the Protectionists.

Under these circumstances, during its first decade the Commonwealth was governed for the most part by the Liberal-Protectionists with Labor support. On many of the great issues Parliament dealt with, the Free Trade Oppositionists fought the government over matters of detail, timing, and emphasis rather than of principle. The Protectionist leader, and prime minister for most of the period, was Alfred Deakin. Native-born son of a Cobb and Co. bookkeeper, Deakin studied law at the University of Melbourne and then became a journalist and a protégé of "King David" Syme, proprietor of the Melbourne *Age*. He was elected to the Victorian parliament in 1880 when he was only twenty-four, and became a cabinet minister three years later. In 1884 he visited the United States to study American irrigation laws and practices. He was the author of much pioneer factory legislation in Victoria and a leading federalist who became the attorney-general in Barton's first (Liberal-Protectionist) Commonwealth government from 1901 to 1903. On Barton's retirement to the High Court Bench, Deakin became prime minister of the Commonwealth for three periods, 1903-1904, 1905-1908, and 1909-1910. If Australians were half as interested in statesmen as they have been in bushrangers, boxers, and race horses, Deakin's name would be a legend in the land he served so well. His fervent nationalism was directed by his strong common sense and by a wide knowledge of men and of other lands in addition to his own. He was a gifted and persuasive orator, though enthusiasm sometimes made him speak too rapidly for his audience. Deeply practical, yet scholarly, sensitive, and astute, he was in his own person a compelling refutation of the ancient myth that "colonials," especially radically inclined ones, were certain to be either bumptious bounders or subservient spiritual adolescents. At Imperial conferences he more than held his own with British prime ministers, and he returned home with his accent and opinions not perceptibly affected by the offer of a knighthood (which he declined), and by much flattery and exposure to aristocratic wealth. The worst that can be said of him is that for many years, in the capacity of anonymous Australian correspondent of the London *Morning Post*, he made not unfavorable reports on his own conduct as Australian prime minister. It was chiefly under his guidance that the first parliaments gave legislative form to the new nation's course.

The most important enactments were concerned with fostering national sentiment and security or with raising living standards for the masses; but, as we have seen, these two policies appeared to many if not most men of the time to be two complementary aspects of the one broad national policy. The now embarrassing "white Australia policy," for instance, was established by the first parliament's Immigration Restriction Act and Pacific Islands Laborers' Act.

Was the policy inspired mainly by nationalistic or by economic motives? Careful examination of all the speeches made in the House of Representatives and the Senate[7] shows that both considerations were present in the minds of almost all members. On balance, arguments based on notions of "racial purity" and the supposedly innate inferiority of colored people predominated over arguments for excluding Africans, Asians, and Polynesians in order to preserve good wages and working conditions; but practically all members who spoke showed that they wanted the legislation for both reasons. It is only fair to remember that the myth of innate white superiority, springing partly from Social Darwinist ideas, was almost universally accepted throughout the western world at the time, especially in English-speaking countries. Australians were by no means uniquely wicked—or ignorant. Rather, they seemed to most literate contemporaries both wise and fortunately placed, when they deported indentured Melanesian laborers from the Queensland sugar plantations and sought to forbid for all time the immigration of any other colored person. If the climate of contemporary opinion be taken into account, the racist arguments were expressed with rather surprising decency and restraint by most members, notably by Deakin. In a much-quoted speech he held that the Japanese, for instance, were not inferior but simply different, indeed that they might well be superior in some respects. Other acts forbade the Commonwealth government to give mail contracts to coastal shipping firms employing any colored labor, and specifically excluded Australia's first inhabitants, the

[7] See M. V. Moore, *Unequal and Inferior: the White Australia Policy in the First Commonwealth Parliament* (Univ. of New England, B.A. thesis, 1962).

aborigines, from the benefits of much welfare legislation. Were they not also black and inferior?

A series of Commonwealth defense acts established the principle that all male citizens were liable to compulsory service and training in the armed forces inside Australia, and in 1907 Deakin's government planned the creation of an Australian Navy which should cooperate with the British Navy in time of war. The Commonwealth took over responsibility for British New Guinea in 1901[8] and for South Australia's neglected Northern Territory in 1910.

In 1908 Deakin's administration passed a bill providing old age and invalid pensions, but farther reaching in its effects was the establishment in 1904 of a Commonwealth Court of Conciliation and Arbitration for settling industrial disputes. Its jurisdiction was limited to industries which operated in more than one state, but all the state governments increasingly tended to follow the federal lead in their own industrial court procedures. The Commonwealth Arbitration Court's second president was Henry Bournes Higgins, a capable and profoundly humanitarian lawyer who had been an independent radical member of the Victorian Parliament until 1900, when he lost his seat because, as many thought, of his public condemnation of Britain's moral position in the Boer War. To understand the importance of the Court's first major decision, we must place it in context. In 1906 Deakin brought forward his policy of "New Protection." In that it consciously aimed equally at national aggrandizement and social welfare, it was perhaps the most characteristic and important legislation of the period. In the following year, by steeply increasing the tariffs on a whole range of manufactured imports, Parliament went far toward making protection the settled fiscal policy of the country. But in accordance with Deakin's humanitarian aims—and of course with Labor's policy—the "New Protection" decreed that Australian manufacturers themselves would be exempt from the new duties, only if each firm could show that its employees were enjoying good wages and conditions as their share of the prosperity fostered by the new tariffs. In the event, though the duties on imported goods remained, the High Court declared that the rest of the legislation was unconstitutional. Yet much the same result was brought about by the action of the Commonwealth Arbitration Court.

In 1907 H. V. McKay Ltd., a large firm of agricultural implement makers, sought exemption from the excise duties imposed by Deakin's still-untested legislation. As president of the Court, Higgins heard a great deal of evidence and refused the exemption, holding that the

[8] See J. D. Legge, *Australian Colonial Policy* (Sydney, 1956).

wages paid by the company were not "fair and reasonable." They were insufficient, he held, to meet "the normal needs of the average employee regarded as a human being living in a civilized community." From an examination of current living costs, Higgins went on to fix the minimum wage which any firm, operating in more than one state, would have to pay even its most unskilled and unenthusiastic employee—as long as he continued on the payroll. Many alterations and modifications to the method of minimum wage fixing have been made since 1907, but the concept of the basic wage itself has remained a fundamental pillar of the Australian way of life. Strong trade unions have helped to ensure that the basic wage is not merely a figure on paper but a reality.

Labor and the "Fusion"

By 1908 both Liberals and Laborites began to feel that their partnership—which had not endured until then without strains and ruptures—had outlived its usefulness. In 1909 Labor formed a short-lived minority administration which was ousted by what seemed to many contemporaries an unnatural fusion between the two middle-class parties. Liberal-Protectionists and conservative Free Traders joined to form the Liberal Party, united at first mainly in its opposition to Labor. Thus, by 1910 the continuing political pattern of the Australian two-party system was established. When the new fusionist government met the House, Deakin was flayed by William Morris Hughes, not then the leader of the Labor Party but easily its most able and venomous member. It was not fair to Judas Iscariot, Hughes said, to compare him with Deakin, for Judas "did not gag the man whom he betrayed, nor did he fail to hang himself afterwards." At the general election of 1910 the electorate showed that it felt there was some substance in Hughes's view of the maneuvers which had led to the fusion. Under the leadership of Andrew Fisher, Labor was returned with an absolute and resounding majority in both houses. The new prime minister was a Scottish coal miner who had immigrated at the age of twenty-three. Steady, some said stodgy, he was yet unswervingly loyal to Labor's moderate ideals. Between 1910 and 1913 his government continued the old Deakinite or "Lib-Lab" policy of welfare-state nationalism, adding here and there a few bravura touches which the opposition denounced as rabid socialism, but which did not impress most electors as such.

The scope of old age and invalid pensions was extended somewhat and maternity allowances were introduced. Government employees were enabled, as those in private industry had already been, to approach the Arbitration Court with grievances. Labor's views on this point had been a source of bitter friction in the defunct Lib-Lab alliance. The Government also imposed a Commonwealth land tax aimed partly, like so much legislation since 1860, at "breaking up the big estates" and thus helping to put the small man on the land. The land tax accomplished little in these directions but proved an acceptable and permanent source of revenue. Easily the most controversial legislation was the creation of the Commonwealth Bank, sponsored most vociferously, if not always most effectively, by King O'Malley, a colorful Tasmanian Labor representative in the federal Parliament from 1901 to 1917. According to circumstances, O'Malley sometimes gave the impression that he had been born in Canada and sometimes in the United States. Similarly, the Commonwealth Bank was to be a "people's bank" which would drive "capitalist banks" out of existence and usher in the millennium, and it was to help and comfort private enterprise too. In fact, from its inception the Commonwealth Bank controlled the note issue and increasingly exercised central banking functions. At the same time, it competed successfully with private banks for all ordinary business and soon became the dominant financial institution of the country.

Fisher's government did much to confirm labor's claim to be the party of Australian—as opposed to generalized British—nationalism. It pushed forward across the treeless desert the railway line to Western Australia, which was completed in 1917. It chose on the Monaro Tableland the beautiful site of the future federal capital, and it conducted a worldwide competition, won by an American architect, Walter Burley Griffin, for the best city plan. The federal Parliament continued to sit in Melbourne until 1927, when the new Parliament House was opened in Canberra by the Duke of York, the future King George VI. The Fisher government also built up the Australian Army and Navy. The latter, consisting by 1913 of a battle cruiser, three cruisers, three destroyers, two submarines, and a number of smaller craft, comprised a large and efficient striking force for a country of little more than four million people, many of whom were inordinately proud of their new fleet. But the Navy was manned by volunteers. The morale of the peace-time land forces was less good, for they were organized on a compulsory basis. Following a report from the distinguished British soldier, Lord Kitchener, called for earlier by the fusionist government, Labor made all males between the age of twelve and twenty-six eligible for military training. Apart from the necessity of school attendance, Australians had never known such regimentation since convict times—and then they had shown marked aversion for peace-time military and police duties. No serious attempt was made to train the younger children, but from the beginning of

1912 onward the Commonwealth prosecuted upwards of 27,000 boys and young men for refusing or evading service.[9] Most of these delinquents were fined, but nearly a quarter of the total were imprisoned. Two brothers called Size, aged eighteen and nineteen, were kept on a diet of bread and water for days on end in a South Australian military jail. When released, they still refused to drill and were again imprisoned. When the First World War broke out a few months later, the Size brothers emphasized the nature of their protest by volunteering for overseas fighting service with the first Australian Imperial Force.

[9] See L. C. Jauncey, *The Story of Conscription in Australia* (London, 1935).

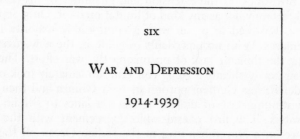

During the whole course of the First World War more Australians than Americans died on the battlefields, and every one of them had volunteered to fight overseas. The total Australian population was less than five million—about equal to that of greater New York City at that time, or to one twentieth of the population of the United States. It is not surprising that the 1914-1918 experience was an almost traumatic one for Australians, comparable in a small way to the United States' Civil War ordeal. After a century of peaceful and ordered development during which rumors of distant wars had hardly troubled a quietly unmilitarist people, events on the other side of the earth suddenly brought death near to practically every Australian home. The utopian dreaming of the past two or three decades was fractured, and with it the illusion that the young nation might forever escape involvement in Old World sins and quarrels. Worse—especially after the broad measure of agreement which had characterized the previous decade or more—the community was divided against itself more bitterly than at any time before or since. After the war Australian life never quite regained its provincial innocence, and even the tempo of material development did not really recover its former momentum for the next twenty years and more. None of this was foreseen, however, when the Great War began on 4 August 1914.

Australians at War

In the federal election campaign being waged at the time, the two parties vied with each other in promising all-out support for the British war effort. Fisher, the Labor leader, undoubtedly spoke for the overwhelming consensus when he promised to help defend the mother country "to our last man and shilling." Fourteen years of national independence and advancement within the Empire seemed to have liquidated the small but vociferous republican minority of the Nineties. Almost everyone, including Irish-Australians, seemed to feel his Britishness as the extension and guarantee of his Australian-ness and certainly not as any kind of limitation on it. On 5 September Labor was returned to power with a comfortable majority in both federal houses. With no precedents to guide it, the new government set about the difficult task of organizing the war effort. The Royal Australian Navy, already a going concern, immediately took over the almost defenseless German portion of New Guinea and then turned to its continuing task of protecting the sea lanes to Britain and in home waters. The first considerable engagement with the enemy took place on 9 November 1914 in the Indian Ocean off the Cocos Islands. The German light cruiser, *Emden*, was caught and sunk in a duel with the slightly better armed Australian light cruiser, *Sydney*. Unrestrained jubilation marked the reception of the news. It was a small battle no doubt, but after all it was the first purely Australian one. In the Boer War small Australian units had been dispersed among larger British formations.

That this practice was not followed in 1914 was largely due to the opposition of the first commander of the Australian Imperial Force, the volunteer army which was recruited to fight overseas. Major-General Sir W. T. Bridges, who had served in South Africa, pressed successfully for the principle that Australian soldiers should not be distributed among British units but should retain their own identity throughout the conflict. Bridges planned to recruit a force of about 20,000 men, but the rush of volunteers at first almost overwhelmed the ability of the skeleton military organization to cope with them. By the end of the war over 330,000 soldiers had actually sailed to Europe or the Middle East as members of the A. I. F.

Australian troops soon came to be known as "diggers"—probably from memories of the gold rush and Eureka as well as from the vast amount of trench-digging in which the men of all armies engaged. By the beginning of 1915 they were established at training camps in Egypt because there were not enough barracks and camp facilities ready for them in England. Thus, accidentally, they took a leading part in the ill-starred Gallipoli campaign. The plan, strongly supported by Winston Churchill, the first lord of the Admiralty, was to seize control of the Dardanelles and thereby open the Black Sea to Allied shipping, bring help to Russia, and perhaps knock the Turkish enemy completely out of the war. It was a good idea, but one doomed to failure by botched tactical planning and insufficient allocation of resources. In the halflight of early dawn on 25 April, thousands of Australia's bravest and best young men stormed ashore on a narrow beach at Gallipoli and clawed their way up an almost perpendicular hillside, in the face of murderous Turkish fire from prepared positions along the crest at the top of the ridge. Those who survived dug in and, with reinforcements, retained their position for eight months until the order for withdrawal was given. More than 10,000 Australian and New Zealand soldiers, including Bridges, as many French soldiers, and nearly three times as many British troops, left their bones in the area for no appreciable military gain. But to have been an "original Anzac"—which is to say a member of the Australian and New Zealand Army Corps at Gallipoli—is still a proud boast for a man and his descendants. Response to the casualty lists was an increase in voluntary enlistments, and 25 April, Anzac Day, has become *the* Australian national day above all others. After the evacuation, some of the A. I. F. stayed to fight on in Palestine until the final Turkish defeat. As the Australian Light Horse under Sir Harry Chauvel, they created their own legend, but the majority of the diggers were shipped to England for regrouping before joining the Allied armies in France.

In the long horror of trench warfare on the western front the five Australian divisions fought valorously. Because they were volunteers, and perhaps also because they were less dependent on, and yet closer to, their officers than the men of European armies, they early came to be regarded as among the best shock troops in the Allied ranks, and were employed accordingly. They suffered more casualties in proportion to the total number of enlistments—nearly 65 per cent—than any other national grouping of British Empire troops. In the initial stages of the final attack on the Hindenburg Line, the Australian contribution was possibly of decisive importance. By then the diggers were commanded by General Sir John Monash, a Jewish Australian, born and educated in Victoria where he took degrees in Arts, Law, and Engineering at the University of Melbourne. Such was his military genius that B. H. Liddel Hart, leading historian of World War One, thought this "unprofessional" soldier might well have become commander-in-chief of the British armies, had the war lasted longer. He played a vital part in planning the attack that led to the final breakthrough and the defeat of Germany, but his civilian service to his country, both before and after the war, was hardly less distinguished. Australians are perhaps more apt than most people to expect little good from high-ranking military officers, but Monash understood and loved his men and was loved in return. His life helps to explain why there is possibly even less anti-Semitism in Australia than in most other English-speaking countries.

Hughes and the Home Front

At home affairs were in charge of a very different type of man— William Morris Hughes, attorney-general in the Labor government until Fisher retired to become high commissioner in London from

October 1915, and thereafter prime minister. Born in Wales in 1864, Hughes emigrated to Australia at the age of twenty and became the most fantastic character—in both senses of that term—so far to distinguish Australian political life. Diminutive, skinny, and gnome-like in appearance, he worked in his youth at a multitude of jobs. He claimed to have been at one time or another—among many other things—a fruit-picker, student-teacher, shearer, cattle-station rouseabout, seaman, cook, tally-clerk, steward, actor, second-hand bookseller and umbrella-mender. But as early as the 1890's he was seeking better fortune in the trade-union and Labor movements. He sat in the New South Wales Parliament from 1894 to 1901 and was thereafter continuously a member of the Commonwealth Parliament until his death in 1952—not, however, after 1917 as a Labor representative. His early experiences may have helped to make him as cunning and as faintly scrupulous as he was able and energetic. Restless, irascible, and ambitious, he drove those near him as hard as he drove himself. It is said that none of the hundreds of male secretaries who worked for him held the position for more than a few months. It is possible to discern throughout the turns and twists of his political career an underlying bias toward nationalist and reformist principles, but much easier to see him manipulating men and ideas toward his own ends. Yet his reputation as a great war leader is largely deserved, and in spite of everything he is more widely known and remembered, if not exactly revered, than any other Australian except the legendary Ned Kelly. Even his political opponents were sometimes half charmed by his murderous wit, the effrontery of his opportunism, and what seemed for so long his sheer indestructibility.

As the war dragged on into its second year, the first flush of adventurous enthusiasm gave way to a mood of dour endurance mixed, as in other countries at war, with some complaining at the irksomeness of censorship, price-fixing, and other necessary but burdensome measures. Government and people alike realized, as casualty lists mounted, that a long and hard trial lay ahead. It was at this juncture early in 1916 that Hughes went to England to see for himself what was happening. His fiery speeches, and his apparent scorn for diplomatic finesse in dealing with dignified and conventional British politicians, appealed to many as typical of the young fighting nation "down under," and Hughes was made much of by the British popular press. This adulation was echoed in Australian newspaper reports of his progress. His fellow-Welshman, David Lloyd George, Britain's wartime prime minister, had nothing to teach Hughes in the art of playing to the gallery. While abroad he also fought hard to persuade the British government that more ships must be diverted to the Australian run to bring badly needed supplies of wheat, wool, and other essentials to the United Kingdom. Finally he bought for the Commonwealth a number of vessels which, as a government-owned line, went some way toward solving the problem. He also became convinced that Australia must speedily introduce conscription for overseas service as Britain had already done.

The Conscription Campaigns

At home universal service leagues had been urging compulsion even before Hughes's departure. The sweeping powers taken to itself by the government in 1914 under the War Precautions Act were probably wide enough to have enabled it to introduce conscription for overseas services by regulation had it wished to do so. Alternatively the Liberal opposition, conscriptionists almost to a man, would certainly have joined with Hughes in passing a new law for the purpose, though the massive Labor majority in the Senate would probably have rejected such a bill and either course would obviously have split the Labor Party and brought down Hughes's government. While all Australians could support the voluntary system a great many Labor voters, and certainly also some Liberals, balked at forcing men to fight and perhaps die on the other side of the world. Some Labor left-wingers were influenced by the internationalist ideals of doctrinaire socialism and others by the lingering isolationist-utopian aspirations of the previous period. Probably more important was the influence of Irish-Australians. Although Catholic enlistments in the A. I. F. were slightly higher, proportionately, than those of men from other denominations, and although some prominent Catholics like Dr. Kelly, Archbishop of Sydney, advocated conscription, the ancient Irish hatred of Britain was fanned into new life by the suppression of the 1916 Easter Rebellion in Dublin. Most important of all, perhaps, was the growing suspicion of trade-union organizations that social advance had not merely been halted, but was being undermined by the government under cover of war emergency measures.

Hughes sought to circumvent the problem by putting the issue to a popular referendum. He was probably right in calculating that, if the people declared for conscription, many of the anti-conscriptionists in Labor's parliamentary ranks would be converted or at least neutralized. The chances seemed good. Most prominent and respectable citizens, the entire daily press of the country, and the still very influential Sydney *Bulletin* passionately advocated compulsion. And most church leaders concurred. The Anglican Synod in Melbourne passed unanimously a resolution certifying that the war was a religious one, that God was on the side of the Allies, and that conscription was

morally necessary. If this were true, the Devil found a powerful advo-
cate in the newly arrived Catholic Coadjutor Bishop of Melbourne,
Dr. Daniel Mannix. At a great public meeting in that city he held
that, though he wished for an Allied victory, Australia could continue
to do its duty nobly under the voluntary system and that in some
respects the conflict was "a sordid trade war." At the end of the meeting a large section of the crowd rose and sang *God Save Ireland.*
Hughes threw everything he had into the campaign while his party
was crumbling round him. He was expelled from the Labor Party by
the extra-parliamentary New South Wales Executive and on the
eve of the referendum several of his cabinet ministers resigned.
Then the people decided, by 1,100,033 to 1,087,557 votes, against
conscription. Anticipating a vote of no confidence in his leadership,
Hughes walked out of a Labor parliamentary caucus meeting, followed by twenty-four others. Some said that the Labor Party had
"blown out its brains," while others talked of rats and sinking ships.
No one seems to have reminded Hughes of his remarks about Deakin
at the time of the fusion. The bitterness was greatest of course in
Labor's own ranks, but the whole community was divided more
deeply than it had been even at the time of the great strikes. Hughes
and his rump of the Labor Party formed a new minority "National
Labor" government with the support of the Liberals, but before long
the two groups fused to form the Nationalist Party with Hughes as
its leader and prime minister.

In the 1917 general election the Nationalists, on a platform of all-
out support for the war effort, were returned to power with a resounding majority; partly, however, because Hughes had promised in
the most explicit terms that conscription would not be introduced
unless it were approved at another referendum. The second referendum campaign in 1917 was even more envenomed than the first, not
least because of the example set by the prime minister. His misuse
of the wartime censorship powers went so far as, on one occasion, to
make the anti-conscriptionist Labor premier of Queensland appear to
have said the opposite of what he in fact had said in a public speech.
In November 1917, when he attempted to address a small crowd in
the Queensland town of Warwick, Mr. Hughes's hat was knocked
from his head by a rotten egg aimed by one Patrick Brosnan—who
was duly fined ten shillings and costs three days later. This incident so
inflamed the prime minister that he at once gave orders for the creation of a Commonwealth Police Force. This body has since pro-
liferated to include a secret security organization of the kind deemed
essential by all civilized countries, which while guarding against foreign spies and domestic traitors also tends to inhibit the expression by

thoughtful citizens of unconventional or unpopular ideas. The addled Warwick egg marked, in a sense, the beginning of the end of Australia's age of innocence.

The second referendum was even more decisively negative than the first. Surprisingly, some thought, even the A. I. F. men in France voted for conscription by only a very slender majority. Perhaps some diggers, knowing the hell of the trenches, could not wish anyone else to be forced into it, but more seem to have been motivated by the *esprit de corps* of a proud force which disdained to beg for unwilling recruits. It is difficult to say certainly why the referenda were defeated but one motive, by no means confined to Labor voters, was the wish of many people to preserve their own freedom of conscience. There were certainly many families like that of the future Liberal prime minister, Robert Gordon Menzies, which felt they had the right to keep one brother at home when the others had all enlisted. The fact that there was at no time any clear and present threat of invasion to Australia itself was probably decisive. Under such circumstances, and with the war being fought on the other side of the earth, one may doubt whether any people ever has, or ever would, impose conscription on itself by popular secret ballot.

Post-War Reconstruction and the Country Party

During the second campaign Hughes had repeatedly promised that he would resign if the referendum were defeated. He did so: but those on both sides of the House who had ingenuously assumed this would mean his stepping down from the prime ministership did not allow for his infinite resourcefulness. Since he was still leader of the majority party, he and his entire cabinet were solemnly sworn in again by the governor-general two days later. Yet when all is said, the incredible Welshman served Australia well. It was largely owing to his energy and persistence that the foundations of an efficient metallurgical industry were laid during the conflict. Pig-iron production, for instance, increased from 47,000 to 332,000 tons between 1913 and 1919. By governmental intervention he did more than any other man to ensure that the basic wool and wheat industries remained stable and productive, and that most of their output was shipped to Britain where it was needed so desperately. At the Versailles Peace Conference he defended ably, if with characteristic truculence and showmanship, what almost all Australians then considered to be vital national interest. C Class mandates were created by the League of Nations largely because of his insistence that Australia must have the substance, if not the legal form, of sovereignty over the ex-German areas of New Guinea. And lest there should be any possible threat to the sacrosanct white Australia policy he fought successfully, though by no means alone, to prevent having a declaration of racial equality incorporated in the League's Covenant.

When the surviving diggers returned home, efforts to help them readjust to peaceful living took two main forms—legislation guaranteeing "preference to returned soldiers," especially in government services, and schemes for settling them on the land. The latter proved, on the whole, costly failures. Preference to returned men was made a reality, at least in the Commonwealth government services, though it often made for lowered efficiency. The Returned Soldiers' League became, however, a very powerful political pressure group as well as an ubiquitous social club which did much for its members and their dependents. Idolized as "the little digger" by many returned men, Hughes continued as prime minister but was not so well trusted by many who had worked with him at closer quarters. His position was threatened particularly by the Country Party, a third grouping in politics which sprang up at this time.

As in the United States at the same period, most people wanted to forget about the war and get back to normal living as quickly as possible. And in spite of the comparatively great development of secondary industries that had taken place, people and governments alike continued to act on the traditionally hallowed belief that Australian development must continue to be primarily rural development. Yet tariff protection of infant manufacturing industries, which inevitably raised farmers' costs, had become the settled policy of both the established political parties. Primary producers in rural Western Australia rebelled first by returning 8 "Country Party" members to their state parliament in 1914. After the war Dr. Earle Page and others launched the Country Party in the eastern states. At the federal election of December 1922 the new party won fourteen seats, giving it the balance of power between the Nationalists and the Laborites, who had won thirty seats each. Page swore that he was ready to cooperate with anybody who would work for rural interests, but in fact the forces behind the Country Party were probably on balance more conservative than those which supported the Nationalists. Working with many members of the Nationalist Party who disliked or distrusted Hughes, Page succeeded in having him ousted from the leadership as the price of Country Party support. The new government was a coalition of the Nationalist and Country parties led by Stanley Melbourne Bruce, a capable Victorian businessman and lawyer who had been educated largely in Britain and was more English in manner than many Englishmen. The Bruce-Page coalition set the pattern of cooperation between the two anti-Labor parties which has lasted ever since in the federal sphere and in most, though not all, of the states. Though tensions between the two groups boil over at times, on the whole they have been at least as successful in maintaining unity in face of their common enemy as Labor has been in containing its own internecine feuds.

These latter were at least as divisive as usual in the period between the two world wars. Battered by the conscription campaigns and the desertion of some of its most capable leaders, the Labor movement was further weakened by a deepening distrust between its political and industrial wings. As political action seemed to have failed them, many trade unionists returned to the idea of militant industrial activity. They were also strongly influenced by the "One Big Union" ideal of the Industrial Workers of the World, a radical socialist organization whose revolutionary doctrines fell on more fertile ground in Australia than in the United States where it originated. One popular I. W. W. song deriding parliamentary and arbitration court procedures did not spare even that incorruptible radical, Henry Bournes Higgins. A Labor candidate for parliamentary honors sings:

> I know the Arbitration Act
>   As a sailor knows his "riggins":
> So if you want a small advance,
>   I'll talk to Justice Higgins.
>
> So bump me into parliament,
>   Bounce me any way;
> Bang me into parliament
>   On next election day.

From its foundation in 1920 the Australian Communist Party rapidly came to displace the I. W. W. as the ideological focus of left-wing agitation: but majority Labor opinion continued overwhelmingly committed to gradualist reform through the parliamentary system. Under these conditions it seemed almost as though the country as a whole distrusted Labor in the vital federal sphere where foreign policy was an issue, while welcoming piecemeal welfare legislation introduced by moderate Labor governments in most of the states. In the twenty-four years from 1917 to 1941 anti-Labor governments ruled the Commonwealth except for the two years 1930-1931; yet the same electors returned Labor governments for much of the time in most of the states.

Under the slogan of "men, money and markets," the Bruce-Page coalition pursued a policy of developing national resources, primarily by tariff and other devices aimed at encouraging private industry.

Protective duties on a wide range of manufactured goods were increased and the uneasiness of the government's Country Party supporters was appeased by the device of extending the protective umbrella to cover also many primary products such as sugar, canned and dried fruits, hops, butter, and grapes. It seemed that there was to be protection for all—except of course for the basic wool and wheatgrowing industries and, as it seemed to many trade union members, for wage-earners. In its concern to keep down costs so that markets abroad could be found for Australian products, the government seemed to its critics to spend more energy in keeping down wages than in demanding greater efficiency from management. To many it seemed that the prewar effort to spread the benefits of protection evenly through the community was being abandoned. But the Commonwealth also spent considerable sums in assisting immigration from the United Kingdom, mainly to promote development but partly also with the white Australia policy in mind. If Australia was to be kept forever a "white" continent, more of its empty spaces would have to be occupied quickly by white men and preferably by Britons. Thus schemes like the groups settlement plan in Western Australia, which sought to transform at a stroke underprivileged British workmen into self-reliant Australian bush-dwellers, were encouraged. Generally speaking the results were even less impressive than those of kindred plans which had been sponsored in the nineteenth century by J. D. Lang and others; but these schemes did bring over 200,000 new citizens to Australia even if few of them became successful farmers. While Labor was, if possible, even more firmly wedded than its opponents to white Australia, it was at best indifferent, and sometimes strongly hostile, to immigration. While unemployment figures remained high, as they did throughout the 1920's, Labor maintained that the government's first duty should be to look after its own citizens by promoting public works instead of bringing in more men to compete for the too few jobs available. The government responded by a public works program which included the building of better main roads in country districts—a project which naturally appealed strongly to its Country Party members; and also by pushing ahead with the building of Canberra whither the federal parliament repaired in 1927. Posterity may hold that the Bruce-Page government's greatest single achievement was the creation in 1926 of the Council for Scientific and Industrial Research, later to be known as the Commonwealth Scientific and Industrial Research Organization, or C. S. I. R. O. This body of first-rate scientists, pure and applied, has wide freedom to carry out all kinds of research which may benefit Australian industry. Its findings are made known freely to all, and it has been of enormous importance to Australian development. Its best-known achievement is probably the "invention" of myxomatosis, a disease which brought the continent-wide rabbit plague under control after the Second World War.

By 1929 ominous signs of coming world depression worried the Nationalist government. All through the decade it had wooed prosperity but at the cost, in the view of the militant trade unions, of the traditional Australian regard for the welfare of working people. There had been many strikes and lockouts, particularly in the transport industries, and the government had passed several measures aimed at disciplining the unions. Now unemployment was growing and yet there seemed no way of increasing the productivity of labor. Rather hastily, and without taking into his confidence all of his own backbenchers, Bruce introduced a bill which would have had the effect of virtually abolishing the whole Commonwealth system of arbitration with its built-in provisions for safeguarding the basic wage. He argued that the state arbitration courts would take over, but the whole Labor movement and some of his own supporters suspected an all-out attack on the national standard of living. Among the back-benchers who had been kept in the dark was Hughes. Scenting revenge for his deposition by Bruce in 1923, he organized the Nationalist and Country Party malcontents and the government was defeated on his no-confidence motion. In the following election there was a landslide to Labor which, however, was left with a minority in the Senate. Hughes's hopes of returning to high office were frustrated by the undiminished hostility of the Labor Party, which did not forget or forgive what it regarded as his betrayal.

The Great Depression

Owing to its heavy dependence on the export of primary products, Australia suffered from the great depression rather earlier and rather more severely than did most countries. For a time nearly 30 per cent of breadwinners were unemployed. Thousands tramped the bush roads again with swag and billy-can,* often ready to work for their keep if only work of any kind could be found. In their bewilderment people did the only thing that offered even the satisfaction of making an angry gesture—and blamed the politicians. The federal government was only the first to be affected. Between 1929 and 1933 every government in the country was thrown out of office by electors reduced to the expedient of "giving the other mob a go—they couldn't be worse." South Australia and the Commonwealth elected their only

* *Swag:* a bushman's rolled up bundle of belongings. *Billy-can:* a tin can for boiling tea.

interwar Labor governments at this time, and Queensland its only anti-Labor one: but politicians understood no more than the electors how to cure the great slump. The main battles were fought in the federal and New South Wales parliaments.

James Scullin, the new prime minister, was a devout Irish-Australian who stood near the middle of Labor opinion. After a lifetime of working for party unity, he could act decisively enough when sure that all sections of the movement were behind him. When a new governor-general had to be appointed, for instance, he virtually forced a most unwilling King George V to name Sir Isaac Isaacs, first native-born Australian to hold the office. Son of poor immigrant Polish Jews, Isaacs had been a Deakinite Liberal, prominent in the federation movement and later a distinguished High Court judge, and in appointing him Scullin was only implementing long-standing Labor policy; but his action caused hysterical outbursts in the daily press and among many Nationalist supporters. Unfortunately the worsening economic problem was susceptible of no such simple solution, and Labor opinion on what should be done varied all the way from the abolition of the capitalist economic system by act of Parliament to obeying exactly the advice of Sir Otto Niemeyer, Bank of England expert on that system, who was invited by the government to Australia to give his views. The only man in Parliament who seemed to have any real understanding of high finance was Scullin's treasurer, the forceful and extremely able E. G. Theodore, known as "Red Ted" both for his views and the color of his hair; but soon after the election he was heavily discredited by the Mungana Mines scandal which cast at least some doubt on his integrity. So the government floundered indecisively while dole-queues lengthened and John Thomas Lang, in October 1930, was elected premier of New South Wales with an enormous Labor majority. Lang or "the Big Fella," as he was called by many admirers, was a tough demagogue, somewhat on the left of parliamentary Labor opinion, though of course strongly anti-Communist. He had already served as premier of his state from 1925 to 1927, and over the years he had built up a personal "machine"—of the type more familiar in American politics—for controlling the New South Wales Labor Party.

Before Lang's return to power, Sir Otto Niemeyer had addressed a premiers' conference called by Scullin in August 1930. At this Melbourne meeting Niemeyer, reflecting the orthodox economic thinking of the time, strongly urged the adoption of deflationary policies. As he saw it, Australia had no alternative but to reduce its artificially high standard of living, not least by cutting salaries and wages. The premiers, however painfully, all agreed to this plan, but most of them did little to carry it out while argument proceeded over ways and means. Lang won power in New South Wales partly by denouncing the "Niemeyer Plan" as a sinister plot of overseas bondholders, and by promising to restore the 44-hour week and the state's civil service salaries, which had been cut by his Nationalist predecessor in office. He also proposed to end unemployment by an extensive program of public works. If money could not be found for these things, then the state should find it by postponing, or if necessary repudiating, interest payments on past overseas borrowings. Many hundreds of thousands of suffering people, not all in his own state, swore by Lang's supposed genius. Slogans such as "Lang is Right," "The Lang Plan," and "Lang is greater than Lenin," were repeated by many and heard by all. Conservatives naturally regarded him as a monster of wickedness, hell-bent on the destruction of all private property and public honor. Feeling grew so intense that for a short time there came into existence an organization of a type unknown in Australia before or since. The self-styled "New Guard" was a quasi-military, quasi-secret, band of "right-thinking" young men from the wealthier suburbs, sworn to preserve the country from Langism. They forcibly broke up some meetings of unemployed and radicals but, as usual in Australian history, there was no loss of life. In March 1932 when Lang was to open the new Sydney Harbor Bridge by cutting a ribbon, a New Guardsman named De Groot spurred forward on horseback and slashed the ribbon with a sword, crying that he opened the bridge "in the name of His Majesty the King and all decent people." Excitement was intense but the police, under the direct control of Lang's government, merely took De Groot to the reception house to be psychiatrically examined.

Meanwhile at a federal election in December 1931 there had been a landslide against Labor, already undermined by another internal split. Joseph Aloysius Lyons, a right-wing Tasmanian Labor member, had resigned from the cabinet over the Mungana scandal and also because he felt the government's vacillating policies were too dangerously radical. With a number of other right-wing Labor members, he negotiated with the Nationalists to reorganize yet again the anti-Labor forces under the style of the United Australia Party, pledged like its predecessors to anti-Communism, praise of private enterprise, and support of respectability. Like Hughes before him, Lyons became leader of the new, or re-named, party and prime minister of Australia from 1932 until his death some months before war broke out in 1939. Cartoonists and comedians made much of the fact that he looked very much like a koala bear, for he had not Hughes' capacity to inspire admiration or hatred.

The Lyons government set about the task of implementing what J. K. Galbraith has since called the "conventional wisdom"[1] of the time. Some months before the election the distracted Scullin government had already been forced to begin carrying out what was essentially the policy of its opponents: a reduction of 20 per cent in all salaries, pensions etc., a roughly commensurate reduction in interest rates, and steep tax increases. The U. A. P. government continued these generally deflationary policies. It also helped to force Lang from office. He went quietly, and the succeeding U. A. P. state government brought New South Wales back into line with the rest of the country. Very gradually the depression eased but there was still widespread unemployment when the Second World War broke out in 1939. Given the prevailing conditions, the deflationary policies adopted in Australia as elsewhere were no doubt inevitable, largely because the conventional economic wisdom of the period backed them vigorously and unanimously. Since then, however, the quite different economic theories of John Maynard Keynes, themselves born of the experience of the great world slump, have become conventional wisdom. It would be implausible to suggest that "the Big Fella" had any deep knowledge of economic theory. Indeed he was once heard to admonish a keen young Labor member discovered reading in the Parliamentary Library—"Reading eh? You'll soon get over that nonsense, son. No time for it here." But ignorance of economic theory in no way distinguished him from all the other political leaders of the day, state and federal, with the possible exception of Theodore. What did distinguish him from them was his passionate advocacy of increased expenditure on public works and other "pump-priming" policies, more inflationary than deflationary in their tendencies; and according to today's conventional economic wisdom, such policies would have been considerably more helpful in combatting the depression than the ones which were generally adopted. We may freely agree that Lang's formulation of his policies was incoherent and emotional rather than logical, and that he would certainly not have been able, even if he had been given the opportunity, to carry them out effectively. Nevertheless, it now seems that, in the broadest sense—that of the direction economic policies should ideally have taken—Lang *was* right after all.

However that may be, the depression experience left a deep and perhaps permanent impression on Australian attitudes. The spectacle of such widespread involuntary unemployment, and even of actual undernourishment, in Australia, while at the same time wheat stacks at the railway sidings were overflowing with unsalable grain, was not

---

[1] *The Affluent Society* (Cambridge, Mass., 1958), *passim*.

forgotten. The traditional belief that the state's first duty is to look after the welfare of all its citizens, more especially the less fortunate among them, was deepened in intensity. After the Great Depression and the Second World War, maintenance of full—not just high—employment became perhaps the greatest single preoccupation of all Australian governments, whatever their political complexion. Between 1945 and 1965 in the Commonwealth as a whole, the number of registered unemployed only very rarely and briefly rose much above 2 per cent of the work force. One important reason seems to have been that the electorate would not readily tolerate a higher rate.[2]

Slow Recovery and War Preparations

The United Australia Party, with the accustomed support of the Country Party, continued to govern until 1940. Though trade recovered slowly, it was hardly an expansive period. After all the government's declared policy, even on the hustings, was one of severe retrenchment and of caution. The U. A. P.'s most positive achievement was probably its courageous trade policy. As we have seen, protection had been the policy of the country ever since federation. Tariffs had risen steadily, right up to and including such emergency depression measures, introduced by the Scullin government, as total prohibition of some imports. There was considerable substance in the Niemeyer view that the national protection policy, with its inevitable tendency to raise internal costs, had placed Australia in an untenable position. The policy could not be simply reversed. Not even the Country Party contained outright free traders any longer but, despite opposition from within its own ranks as well as from Labor, the government did lower tariffs here and there throughout the Thirties, while it sought reciprocal trade agreements with other countries and particularly with other British Empire countries. Under the Ottawa Agreements of 1932 lower, preferential tariffs were extended to a wide range of British, Canadian, and other Empire goods. These policies, despite the passionate objections of many Australian manufacturers, were certainly beneficial in the long run if only because they forced Australian secondary industry to become somewhat more efficient and competitive.

Under its general anti-Communist mandate the government sought to encourage what it regarded as right thinking at home and to protect citizens from impure or dangerous thoughts from abroad. On the whole, these efforts brought more discredit upon itself than on its opponents. A censorship of imported books, administered largely by

[2] Russel Ward, "'Frontierism' and National Stereotypes," in *Canadian Historical Association, Annual Report* (Ottawa, 1965).

only modestly literate customs officials, sought to keep out of the country Marxist works and also such purely literary masterpieces as James Joyce's *Ulysses*. In 1934 Egon Kisch, a learned Czech author, came to Australia to attend a Melbourne antiwar conference. The government declared that he had affiliations with Communist organizations and forbade him to land. Kisch jumped onto the wharf, broke his leg, and was taken to a hospital in Melbourne. The government decided to deport him under a clause of the Immigration Restriction Act which had been designed to safeguard the white Australia policy. Instead of saying openly that a man could not land because of the color of his skin, this clause empowered officials to give a prospective visitor or migrant a dictation test in any European language. Its obvious intention was to enable officials to use a language unknown to the testee who could then be barred—technically on some vague suggestion of his illiteracy. Such was Kisch's reputation for scholarship, however, that the government thought it wise to give him a dictation test in Gaelic, the almost extinct language of the Highland Scots. Kisch duly failed. "Australia is disgraced," wrote the nationally respected scholar and essayist, Walter Murdoch. Later the High Court found that Gaelic was not a European language within the meaning of the act. Possibly even more damaging to the government's reputation was the case of Mrs. M. M. Freer. This respectable Englishwoman was given a dictation test in Italian and kept out of the country for nearly a year—for no other reason than that a minister of the Crown had listened to a personal friend, who told him he believed that Mrs. Freer might "break up an Australian home." Such events demonstrated that the broad streak of petty provincialism which has so often been associated with Australian nationalism was by no means confined to one side in Australian politics.

But even this strong tendency toward isolationism was not completely proof against Hitler's preparations for another war. Compulsory training had been abandoned by the Labor government at the beginning of the depression, ostensibly as an economy measure but possibly more in fact because of Labor's deep-seated distrust of any kind of militarism. As the international situation darkened the U. A. P. government did little to strengthen the land forces but began to spend a little more money on naval rejuvenation. Labor, at the official parliamentary level, advocated instead the creation of a strong air force, partly because its leaders felt that an air arm, in view of Australia's remoteness from Europe, was in its nature a more defensive weapon than a navy. But in fact both parties, though for different reasons, found it almost impossible to formulate a coherent foreign policy. The electorate, as always in the past except during the actual fighting of World War One, continued to be vastly more concerned with bread-and-butter domestic issues. Almost everyone was horrified at the Nazis' bestial treatment of the Jews, and there was widespread support for Lyons' decision in 1938 to welcome 5,000 refugees a year from Nazi tyranny; but what should be done to meet the military threat of Nazism seemed a more difficult but less urgent question. Like conservative parties everywhere, the U. A. P. was divided between its fear of the revisionist aims and violent, larrikin methods of the Fascist powers, and its hope that all this explosive force might in the end be spent on weakening or destroying Russian Communism. Like "socialist" parties everywhere, Labor was divided between its hatred of all that Fascism stood for, and its strong traditional attachment to ways of peace, which inhibited it from preparing effectively for war. Thus, the U. A. P. prepared half-heartedly for war, while at the same time making conciliatory and appeasing noises toward Fascism: and Labor for the most part denounced Fascism in unmeasured terms, while at the same time it was even less willing than its opponents to underwrite really effective war preparations.

The paradox was vividly illustrated in 1938 when the U. A. P. attorney-general, Robert Gordon Menzies, acquired his sobriquet of "Pig-Iron Bob." In June, to scotch a Japanese scheme for importing large quantities of iron *ore* from Western Australia, the government imposed an embargo on its export from the whole country. Yet considerable quantities of *pig* and *scrap* iron continued to be shipped to Japan from eastern ports. The militant Waterside Workers' Union at Port Kembla refused to load such cargoes on the grounds that they would help Fascism and might be returned to Australia later in the form of Japanese bombs. Menzies threatened to coerce the union under some provisions of the Crimes Act, and he had the courage to face the men on the wharves personally to explain the government's point of view. Nevertheless, the whole incident was a great embarrassment to the U. A. P. for many years, particularly after Pearl Harbor. At bottom the whole foreign policy debate had a faint air of unreality about it because everyone knew that in fact Australia, as in the past, would simply follow Britain's lead and go to war with her if things became really serious. And nearly everyone who thought at all of such matters agreed that this was both natural and right.

The "Mean Decades"?

In the arts there was a reaction between the wars against outbackery and "aggressive Australianism," healthy in itself but leading nowhere very much else at the time. On the whole the cultural achievement compares poorly with that of the thirty years before the

First World War. Compared with that of the Heidelberg school,[3] most painting was derivative and pleasant rather than new and robust. In literature "Henry Handel Richardson" and Christopher Brennan reached the first rank, but their work belongs as much to the earlier period as to the interwar one. In their anxiety to break away from the horse-and-stockwhip tradition of the Nineties, many of the poets emphasized a neo-paganist, art-for-art's-sake approach which was a natural reaction from the prevailing shallow materialism, but which was also curiously reminiscent of the literary attitude popular thirty years earlier in the England of the "naughty Nineties." And the best works of Kenneth Slessor, perhaps the most considerable poet of this *Vision* group, owe little to its declared theories. Indeed a poem like his "Country Towns" does not so much repudiate the earlier tradition as use it in a new, wry way to say something more permanently worthwhile about Australia than was implied by the contemporary cry for "men, money and markets."

> Country towns, with your willows and squares,
> And farmers bouncing on barrel mares
> To public-houses of yellow wood
> With "1860" over the doors,
> And that mysterious race of Hogans
> Which always keeps the general stores. . . .
>
> At the School of Arts, a broadsheet lies
> Sprayed with the sarcasm of flies:
> "The Great Golightly Family
> Of Entertainers Here To-night"
> Dated a year and a half ago,
> But left there, less from carelessness
> Than from a wish to seem polite.

In the 1920's Katharine Susannah Prichard wrote two good novels, *Coonardoo* and *Working Bullocks*, and the following depression decade inspired some worthwhile "realist" writing by Vance Palmer and others. Xavier Herbert's *Capricornia* will probably always find readers and Kyle Tennant's *The Battlers* deserves to. But for the most part the writers themselves were among the first to contrast their own barren time with what had gone before.

In what most Australians regarded as a far more important sphere, there was less to despond about. They continued, they thought, to lead the world in cricket, tennis, and swimming. It was in this period that the swimming stroke known elsewhere as the "Australian crawl"

[3] See p. 83.

was adopted by most other nations, as the "Australian ballot" had been earlier. Surf and life-saving clubs, manned entirely by volunteers, multiplied enormously, and an Australian who could not swim came to be regarded as something of a cripple. On 6 February 1938, when three freak waves in succession swept thousands of surfers out to sea off Sydney's Bondi Beach, the local lifesavers rescued from drowning over 200 people in half an hour or so and only five lives were lost. The Adelaide brothers Ross and Keith Smith, Queensland's Bert Hinkler, and the great "Smithy," Sir Charles Kingsford Smith, ranked with America's Lindberg as pioneers of intercontinental air navigation. And neither the Great War nor the Great Depression was allowed to interfere with the most important national ritual apart from Anzac Day, the running of the Melbourne Cup on the first Tuesday of November. Indeed Australia's greatest horse, Phar Lap (actually raised in New Zealand), won the race in 1930 and competed in the following year only to die shortly afterward, darkly, some insisted on believing, in America: but his body was brought home, stuffed, and reverently mounted in the Melbourne Museum, while his heart was enshrined at Canberra.

In more conventionally important areas there was some advance in the mid-Twenties, but before and afterward the economy was hardly more than static even in "good" years. In fact, at the height of the modest post-war "boom" in 1926, 7 per cent of trade-union members were unemployed. During the depression that followed the total Australian population actually declined by more than 10,000 between 1931 and 1935. The C. S. I. R. O. was founded in 1927 and its charter was broadened ten years later to include research in fields relevant to secondary industry. The Australian Broadcasting Commission was founded in 1932. Almost at once it began to raise the standard of public taste in music and the arts generally by its competition with privately owned radio corporations. And in the late 1930's, by admitting a number of graduate cadets into the Commonwealth government departments, the U. A. P. did something toward raising the generally low standard of efficiency in the civil service. But this above all others was the time when mechanics' institutes and schools of arts, founded so hopefully in the previous century, fell into hopeless decay; and it was hard to see what, if anything, was to take their place. The number of universities, university teachers, and students remained almost at the low prewar levels—except in Western Australia, where an unusually beautiful complex of university buildings was begun. The Western Australian wheat industry, too, really became important in the Twenties.

R. M. Crawford has characterized the 1920's as Australia's "mean decade," and few will disagree with his belief that the meanness derived in an important measure from the First World War's effects.[4] Over sixty thousand of this small nation's most generous and gifted men, those who might have led the way, fought and died far from home in that war. But few will agree with Crawford's further suggestion that things began to look up quite remarkably in the late 1930's. In fact, the whole interwar period, compared with those which preceded and followed it, was an uncertain, cautious, and shabby era. Honorable exceptions notwithstanding, most political and other leaders, made timid by their memories of the bitter conscription troubles and by the vivid if distant specter of Bolshevism, sought to survive rather than to create. War had shattered the possibly naïve, but nonetheless constructive, idealist national mood of the previous decades without substituting anything very positive in its place. Men honored the fallen and would continue to do so, but were not at all clear about what—other than the continued existence of Australia as a sovereign state—they had died for. So the fire went out of the vision which had inspired so many men of the previous generation, while contemporary experience suggested little more than a disillusioned continuance of the habitual attitudes from which the vision had sprung. Recovery and advance to a more mature national stance was to be the work of the diggers' children rather than of the survivors of the war to end all wars.

[4] *An Australian Perspective* (Madison, 1960), pp. 61-70.

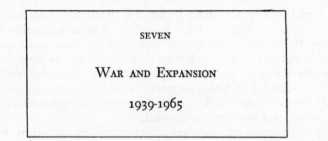

When war began on 3 September 1939 the national mood
was strikingly different from that of August 1914. There was no wild
enthusiasm or false optimism—nor, for that matter, much sign of
panic or profound fear. Men knew now what war was like. They
knew too that, since Japan was a member of the tripartite Axis bloc,
this war might well be fought in part on Australian soil. At best a
long and bitter trial lay ahead. On the evening of that day the new
prime minister, R. G. Menzies, who had succeeded to the leadership
on Lyons' death only five months earlier, spoke to the nation on the
radio. He said that, since the Nazi invasion of Poland had forced
Great Britain to declare war on Germany, Australia was also at war.
He spoke calmly and sadly but resolutely, thereby matching exactly
the feeling of most citizens—though he was not fated to lead them
through most of the conflict.

Menzies and the First Year of War

Born in a small country town in the Victorian wheat belt, Menzies
was educated at Wesley College in Melbourne and later at the University there. He studied law and practiced it very successfully for
ten years before being elected to the Victorian Parliament in 1928.
He rapidly became deputy-premier of the state, but in 1934 decided
to transfer his ambitions to the larger sphere of federal politics. As
the United Australia Party candidate he was elected by the voters
of Kooyong, a rather fashionable Melbourne suburban area, and they
have returned him continually to the House of Representatives ever
since. Menzies was endowed with a brilliant mind and a dominating
personality, and his career makes an almost unbroken success story
from his first days at school until he became prime minister at the
age of only forty-five. His fall from power during the war years was
so humiliating that few then imagined a recovery was possible. Yet
such was the man's stamina that he brought his party, under yet
another name, back to power in 1949 and was still serving as prime

minister in 1965. He is a superb orator and parliamentary debater, and a platform speaker who thrives on interjections; his colleagues were forced to realize that his leadership was indispensable to the success of the party, yet few of them felt for him much personal warmth. For conservative voters he came in the end to possess almost the *mana* of a tribal god: he was powerful, wise, well-bred, witty and, above all, sound. Few Labor supporters denied his tremendous ability, but to them he appeared also as unscrupulous, opportunistic, condescending, and insufferably arrogant.

The government at once set about enrolling volunteers for the Second A. I. F. As Japan remained at peace the decision was made, though with some misgivings, to send the soldiers at first to the Middle East where their fathers had fought. In January 1940 the first contingent sailed from Sydney Harbor, some of them traveling in giant liners from the North Atlantic run such as the *Queen Mary*, the like of which had never been seen previously in Australian waters. With the fall of France in June 1940 and Italy's entry into the war, the decision seemed to have been the right one. Australia's airmen shared in the epic defense of Britain while her soldiers and sailors fought in the Mediterranean and in North Africa, Syria, Greece, and Crete. The A. I. F. shared the task of driving Mussolini's legions out of Egypt and well back into the Italian colony of Libya, but when the Germans entered the Mediterranean war the diggers were in turn driven back to Egypt, leaving the heroic garrison of "desert rats" as a strong point behind the enemy lines at Tobruk. Australians formed the rear guard in Greece and Crete where many men were taken prisoner as well as lost in battle. Syria, however, was cleared of Hitler's Vichy-French allies. Australian naval ships took part in the decisive Battle of Cape Matapan, which gave Britain precarious control of the Mediterranean Sea. But ominously Japan began to move south, first into French Indo China, and other Australian forces were sent to Malaya, to points in the Dutch East Indies, and to Darwin and Rabaul.

Curtin and the Japanese Attack

Meanwhile the U. A. P.–Country Party government seemed to be losing internal cohesion and popular support. The general election of September 1940 returned thirty-six government candidates and the same number of Labor members, so that the Menzies ministry depended entirely on the support of two Independents—one, A. W. Coles, a chain-store magnate and the other, Alex Wilson, the representative of a small-farming area in Victoria. As the war situation grew worse Menzies' leadership was questioned more and more sharply, not only by the country at large, but also by his own colleagues. At the end of August 1941 Arthur Fadden, the Country Party leader, replaced Menzies as prime minister, but otherwise the cabinet remained unchanged. It was soon clear, however, that Fadden held even less control over the situation and his government lasted for little more than a month. On 3 October John Curtin, the leader of the Labor opposition, moved a vote of no confidence. Coles and Wilson were disgusted by the personal jealousies in the government's ranks as well as by its apparent fumbling. They undoubtedly reflected faithfully the feeling of the majority of the people outside parliament when they crossed the floor to vote with Labor. The Curtin ministry was confirmed in office with a huge majority in both houses at the next general election in September 1943. Ever since federation Labor had claimed to be the party of national Australian patriotism, just as the anti-Labor parties had always laid more stress on the importance of generalized imperial, or British, patriotism. It seems that the electorate recognized some validity in these two party images, for as the Japanese moved south it became painfully clear that the time-honored concept of complete reliance on Britain might no longer serve. If the dreadful choice between defending Britain or Australia first had to be made, naturally there could be no doubt about the majority decision.

The new prime minister combined in his own person much that was characteristic of the Australian Labor movement. Born in Victoria in 1885, Curtin made his home in Western Australia from 1917 onward. Brought up in an Irish-Catholic family, he lost his religious faith as a young man when he embraced socialist ideals. Through the long work-a-day years of battling as a trade-union organizer and a Labor journalist, through all the compromises and disillusionment which form such a large part of politics and of growing up, he never quite lost the vision he had seen in his youth. Quiet-spoken, thoughtful, and unquestionably sincere, he was not, as Menzies was, an obviously impressive personality. Some thought him weak and vacillating. Yet he did more than perhaps any other single person to reunite his party and movement after the splits and catastrophes of the depression years, and as prime minister during the darkest days Australia had ever known he gave firm and inspiring leadership. His political opponents sometimes derided him for having been a strong anti-conscriptionist with pacifist leanings during the First World War, but more often they were inhibited by the fact that their own leader, R. G. Menzies, had resigned his commission in the Melbourne University Regiment on the outbreak of that conflict.

The new government had hardly been sworn into office when the nation's fortitude was taxed to the utmost. The cruiser *Sydney* was lost with all hands in the Indian Ocean only a few hundred miles from Fremantle, Curtin's home town. On 7 December the Japanese made their treacherous attack on Pearl Harbor. Thereby American might was enlisted on the side of the Allies, but at the time it seemed that, with much of the United States' Navy sunk in the sneak attack, Australia was more open than ever to an enemy invasion. Hong Kong, Borneo, the Philippines, and Rabaul in New Britain—just to the north of New Guinea—fell to the Japanese. The Australian Eighth Division took part in the stubborn fighting retreat in Malaya, but it seemed that nothing could stop the enemy. Two months before the surrender of Singapore on 15 February 1942, the only major gesture that beleaguered Britain was then able to make in the Indian Ocean–Pacific area ended in disaster. Two of the most formidable ships in the Royal Navy, the *Prince of Wales* and the *Repulse*, were ignominiously sunk by vastly superior Japanese air power off the Malayan coast. The 15,000 Australians on Singapore Island were driven, with their British and Indian comrades, into prisoner-of-war cages. The day, so often prophesied by romantic Australian writers, when the country would stand alone to face an Asian invasion, seemed to have arrived.

The American Alliance

The effect of these events on long-standing Australian assumptions cannot be overestimated. Ever since the first landing at Sydney Cove, most men had taken it for granted in their hearts that Australian security was an indivisible part of British security and that Britain, particularly the British Navy, was naturally unconquerable. For a generation Australians had been brought up to believe that the Singapore Naval Base was the impregnable pivot of Australian security *vis-à-vis* Japan. All this was swept away in a few terrible weeks. It has often been said that the Australian nation was born at Gallipoli. It is certainly no less true to say that Australia came of age at Singapore. Whether she would have to face the Japanese alone during the next few critical months only time could tell, but it was certain that thenceforward she must be responsible for her own destiny in a way that had hardly occurred to most citizens in the past. Yet old habits die hard. During the Japanese advance in Malaya two of the three Australian divisions fighting in the Middle East were hastily withdrawn to reinforce the Singapore garrison: but these diggers were still on the high seas when the fortress fell. Churchill demanded that they be diverted to bolster the defense of Burma and India—and his view was shared by some Opposition members at Canberra. Churchill seems to have been both surprised and angry at Curtin's inflexible insistence that these seasoned troops were needed to kill Japanese nearer their own homes.

It was against this background that the prime minister made his historic appeal for American help. In some ways the words seemed shocking at the time, even to many dyed-in-the-wool Labor men, but they were less shocking than the position Australia was in. The speech was overwhelmingly endorsed by public opinion:

> Without any inhibitions of any kind, I make it quite clear that Australia looks to America, free of any pangs as to our traditional links or kinship with the United Kingdom. . . . We know . . . that Australia can go and Britain can still hold on. We are, therefore, determined that Australia shall not go, and we shall exert all our energies towards the shaping of a plan with the United States . . . which will give our country some confidence of being able to hold out until the tide of battle swings against the enemy.

Naturally America was glad to have Australia as a base from which to mount and launch a counterattack on the Japanese. Soon General Douglas MacArthur, escaped hero of American resistance in the Philippines, was established in Melbourne in supreme command of Allied forces in the whole Southwest Pacific area. His imperious style was not such as to appeal to most Australians, but none questioned his dedicated ability and his superb fitness for the post. That two men so different in nature and background as he and Curtin became friends is some measure of the stature of each. In spite of some friction, springing largely from the much higher rates of American military pay, U. S. servicemen were naturally welcomed with open arms in Australia and the alliance worked uncommonly well.

Nevertheless, after the Pearl Harbor disaster American strength could not be brought to bear overnight. For some months it was touch-and-go whether there would be a Japanese landing in force. The enemy took northern New Guinea and many of the Solomon Islands. Darwin, Broome, Wyndham, and other northern Australian mainland ports were bombed. Ships were sunk within sight of the New South Wales coast by the Japanese Navy, and one night ferry passengers watched a lively exchange of gunfire in the middle of Sydney Harbor which had been penetrated by enemy midget submarines. At this period one keyed-up citizen, wakened and brought to the front door of his flat by an air-raid warden, knocked out the latter with a right to the jaw before realizing that he was not a member of a Japanese landing party.

The first sign of a turn in the tide came in May 1942 when a combined American-Australian fleet checked and drove back a Japanese naval force near the southern end of the Solomon Island chain. In this series of associated actions, which came to be known as the Battle of the Coral Sea, Australia lost another powerful cruiser, the *Canberra*. In June the main American fleet clinched this success by its decisive defeat of the Japanese at the Battle of Midway. Meanwhile enemy troops had crossed the precipitous Owen Stanley Range, mountainous backbone of New Guinea, and were approaching the main Australian base on the island's southern coast at Port Moresby, only a few hours sailing time from the mainland. In August at Milne Bay, near the eastern tip of New Guinea, a scratch force of Australians won the distinction of inflicting on Japanese land forces their first real defeat of the war. In a week of savage, hand-to-hand, jungle fighting, the invaders were met, stopped, and smashed. In the following month other diggers halted the enemy advance on Port Moresby and then, step by step, drove the Japanese back again over the Owen Stanleys. The war in the Pacific was far from won, but from this time onward an invasion of Australia seemed increasingly unlikely. By the end of the year the tide had turned on the other side of the world also. The Australian Ninth Division helped to smash German and Italian power in North Africa at the decisive Battle of El Alamein, while at the same time the Russian armies at bay routed the Germans at Stalingrad. From November 1942 onward the Axis powers were on the defensive and total Allied victory, however long and hard the road, was in sight.

The Home Front in World War II

At home in Australia political and other events furnished in many ways a striking contrast with those of the First World War. In politics the anti-Labor parties were weakened and discredited while Labor grew in unity and stature—just the opposite of what had happened twenty-five years earlier. Then the question of conscription for overseas military service had been the rock which split the Labor Party and the nation, whereas during World War Two the Curtin government imposed conscription with hardly a ripple of protest. True, Opposition members denounced the amendment to the Defense Act by which conscripts were required to serve overseas only as far away from Australian shores as the equator on the north and a roughly equivalent distance to east and west of the continent; but these boundaries covered the area where in fact most of the fighting in defense of Australia was taking place. On the left and within the government's own ranks hardly a voice dissented strongly. Of course this wide measure of agreement was to a great extent imposed by the imminent peril of invasion. It would have been difficult even for doctrinaires to maintain that home defense ought to mean waiting till the enemy had actually landed on Australian soil. Minor reasons were the fact that those sections of the community traditionally opposed to conscription were also traditionally pro-Labor and so more willing to trust "their government" with sweeping powers, and that the Australian Communist Party's influence—by no means negligible in the trade unions during the war years when Russia was doing so much to bleed the common enemy—was of course solidly behind the war effort.

Australians also accepted, with possibly less grumbling than such measures would have evoked in most free countries, a high measure of government direction in civil life. Essington Lewis, the extremely able manager of the country's greatest metal corporation, the Broken Hill Proprietary Company, was appointed director-general of munitions. Machine tools, precision optical goods, machine guns, and even airplanes—all previously regarded as beyond the technological capacity of Australian industry—were soon being produced in large quantities. A Department of War Organization of Industry diverted the use of all possible plants to war purposes, while such organizations as the Allied Works Council and the Civil Construction Corps conscripted labor for the building of airports, port facilities, and other urgent tasks. Clothing and basic foods were rationed. Tobacco and liquor grew so scarce as to be almost unobtainable at times by civilians, while gasoline rationing almost banished private cars from the roads. Many of these controls were established by the U. A. P. government, but the war situation enabled Labor to use them more vigorously and to add others. Together they helped Australia's seven and a half million people to provision their million-odd servicemen and to find food, and some equipment too, for the hundreds of thousands of American troops in the Southwest Pacific area. Toward the end of the war the government also introduced a wide range of social benefits which included university scholarships for able young people and ex-servicemen, help for unemployed and sick people, free provision for all of certain life-saving drugs, and increased subsidies for hospitals.

Rehabilitation and Expansion

The prime minister died in harness before the final victory and was succeeded by Joseph Benedict Chifley, who had been treasurer in Curtin's cabinets. A year later in the election of September 1946 Labor lost only six seats, and two of these were to independent Labor members, one a left-wing dissident and the other J. T. Lang, returning like a ghost from the past to badger the party he could no longer control. The Chifley government initiated a number of measures which were to have far-reaching effects on the whole pattern of Australian life. Ever since federation the Commonwealth had tended to gain power at the expense of the states, and this process had gathered momentum during the war—not least by the "uniform taxation" arrangements of 1942 under which the Commonwealth assumed exclusive power to levy income tax, some of which was handed back to the states in annual grants or "reimbursements." War also underlined the essential unity of the nation. Afterward men were somewhat less concerned about state rights and more accustomed to look to Canberra for broad national initiatives.

Demobilization of servicemen and their rehabilitation into civil life proceeded smoothly and quickly, amazingly so compared with the equivalent performance at the end of World War One. Many men returned to their old jobs; for others subsidized training for trades and professions was provided. The war had practically ended the notion that Australia must forever remain a land of farmers and graziers. Land-settlement schemes catered for only a small minority of the demobilized diggers, but these men were given every reasonable help and were almost uniformly successful. Partly in order to accommodate the wave of ex-servicemen who wanted professional training, the Commonwealth government moved into the field of tertiary education. Old universities expanded their facilities, new universities were set up, and the Australian National University, conceived as primarily a post-graduate research and training institute, was founded in Canberra. Private home-building had almost ceased during the war. Commonwealth and state government agreements to alleviate this shortage were not so successful. For a time the term "squatter" came to mean not a wealthy grazier, but an ex-serviceman forced to "squat" with his family in almost any unoccupied building; but government action did help to keep the cost of housing lower than it would otherwise have been during the post-war housing famine. Perhaps the most imaginative scheme was that launched for developing the resources of the Snowy Mountains area on the border between New South Wales and Victoria. This giant undertaking has been continued and expanded by the succeeding Menzies governments. When completed, millions of tons of water, which had run to waste annually in the Pacific, will be used to supply much of Australia's needs for electric power. In addition, the water will be diverted through tunnels so as to flow out onto the dry western plains of New South Wales for irrigation.

The greatest breaks with the past were made, however, in the fields of immigration and foreign policy. There had been much assisted migration throughout Australian history, but the scheme introduced by Arthur Augustus Calwell, Chifley's minister for immigration, was unique both in its scope and in that it was sponsored so enthusiastically by Labor. The war had jolted everyone into realizing that in the future Australia would have to rely on her own resources for defense, and for this the greatest single need was more Australians. More people were not less important for a higher rate of economic growth and increased prosperity. Human decency also played some part in making men want to help displaced persons and other victims of the war in Europe. In the past Labor had opposed, or at best tolerated, assisted immigration on the ground that the government's first duty was to find work at reasonable wages for those already in the country. But there had been no appreciable unemployment since 1940. Jobs were more plentiful than ever immediately after the war and the Labor movement—possibly with some muted misgivings—decided to trust its own government to maintain full employment indefinitely. More surprising was the agreement of all political parties that about half of the immigrants might be European, but non-British, in origin, and most surprising of all to anyone who knew the provincial xenophobia of Australians before the war was the generally friendly way in which they now accepted the newcomers. Abusive or contemptuous terms like "Dago" and "Reffo" (refugee) gave way, not just at an official level but in general usage, to "New Australian"; though "Pommy" tended to stick more tenaciously to British immigrants, partly to distinguish them from other New Australians who, as an Irishman might have put it, were after all so much newer. Between 1945 and 1965 well over two million immigrants came to the country and the total population rose from 7,500,000 to 11,000,000.

Herbert Vere Evatt, attorney-general and minister for external affairs from 1941 to 1949, had stepped down from the High Court bench in order to contest a Sydney suburban seat in the Labor interest. An intellectual and an idealist, he believed passionately in the importance of civil liberty at home and of the rule of law in international affairs. Some thought him insufficiently realistic for the hurly-burly of political life, and others pointed to streaks of instability and of almost child-like vanity in his character. Yet his integrity was unquestioned and his legal brilliance proverbial. The latter was the subject of one of those asides which occasionally break the tedium of proceedings in the House of Representatives. Menzies, himself no mean lawyer, was "confessing" in his loftiest and most ironic style his "inability" to understand the legal reasoning behind a Labor argument. "Never mind Bob—Bert Evatt can," interjected E. J.

Ward, member for East Sydney and one of the very few men capable of ruffling the prime minister's customary urbanity. When at the end of the war the Indonesians revolted against their Dutch masters, Evatt and the government sympathized with the rebels and did nothing to hinder a continentwide wharf-laborers' boycott of Dutch ships. Probably most Australians wished the Indonesians well, though many Opposition supporters were scandalized at the very idea of those whom some were old-fashioned enough to call "natives" being helped to oppose "white men," no matter what the circumstances. On the whole Australians encouraged Indonesian independence partly from genuine belief in the natural right of every people to govern itself, and partly too from motives of self-interest. Evatt was by no means the only person to realize that the days of European rule over Asia and Africa were numbered, that in the future Australia would have to learn to deal with neighboring Asian governments, and that she would need all the Asian friends she could get.[1] Despite its implicit contradiction of the white Australia policy—to which both Labor and anti-Labor parties remained passionately attached—this liberal, internationalist policy was warmly advocated by Evatt at the early meetings of the United Nations Organization. As the candidate of a bloc of small and medium powers he was elected president of the U. N. General Assembly in 1948.

Post-War Politics

The most controversial legislation of the time was the Banking Act of 1947, which set out to nationalize the whole banking system. In Chifley's view this was necessary as a safeguard against the possibility of future depressions; but Australia had in fact never been so prosperous, and conservatives regarded the banking legislation as an almost revolutionary attack upon private enterprise. The government also sought to nationalize air services, but both measures were ruled unconstitutional by the High Court. A government-owned airline, Trans-Australian Airways, was set up in competition with private companies, however, and it, with the government-owned Australian overseas airline, Qantas, has maintained since a record of safety and efficiency second to none in the world. At about the same time Churchill's "iron-curtain" speech at Fulton, Missouri, gave impetus to the revived wave of anti-Communism which was sweeping all western countries. In Australia as elsewhere people were tired of war-time restrictions and controls some of which, like a modified form of gasoline rationing, still survived. In the midst of prosperity and expansion a bitter

[1] J. D. Legge, *Indonesia* (Englewood Cliffs, 1965), in "The Modern Nations in Historical Perspective" series, R. W. Winks, gen. ed.

coal strike caused power shortages which, on some nights, plunged great cities into darkness. People were unpleasantly reminded of the war-time blackout. At the nadir of U. A. P. fortunes in 1944 Menzies had taken the leading part in yet another reorganization of the anti-Labor forces under the new (or refurbished) banner of the Liberal Party. He now promised to abolish gasoline rationing and other troublesome restrictions on private enterprise, and to smash the influence of Communism in the trade unions and elsewhere by making the Communist Party an illegal organization. At the election of 1949 the Liberal and Country parties came back to power again with a comfortable majority. Within a few months Australian volunteers were again fighting overseas, this time in Korea. True to its election promise, the new government passed in 1950 a Communist Party Dissolution Bill.

The new act gave power to declare the Australian Communist Party, and other bodies deemed to be affiliated with it, illegal organizations whose property should be forfeited to the Commonwealth. It also barred Communists from employment in the Commonwealth Government services and from holding offices in key trade unions, and it gave the government power to "declare" citizens to be Communists. Contrary to the ancient principle of British law, the onus of disproving the charge was placed squarely on the accused or "declared" persons. In speaking to the bill in the House, the prime minister anticipated its passage a little by "declaring" twenty or so Communist trade-union officers whose names had presumably been supplied to him by the security services. The fact that some were not Communists, and that one was neither a Communist nor even a trade-union member, did not reassure the large body of moderate opinion which was strongly anti-Communist but troubled by the idea of entrusting such arbitrary powers to any government. The bill was passed but immediately challenged in the High Court by the Communist Party and by some powerful trade unions such as that of the waterside workers. Labor was a little half-hearted in its opposition to the bill, partly for fear of being branded with guilt by association and partly because some Catholic Labor men were at least as illiberal on this matter as was the Liberal Government. Nevertheless Evatt, in his private legal capacity, argued the case for the unions before the High Court, which found the bill unconstitutional in March 1951.

The government then decided to seek a constitutional amendment to give it the necessary power for passing its anti-Communist legislation, and accordingly prepared for a nationwide referendum on the subject. At this point Chifley died suddenly and Evatt succeeded to the leadership of the Opposition. Despite the latter's zeal for a No vote, the referendum campaign was not fought strictly on party lines. Government members and practically all newspapers and radio commentators urged the electors to vote Yes, and some Labor men joined them—if only by their significant silence upon the issue; but as the campaign warmed up a good many prominent citizens not identified at all with party politics, including some who probably normally voted conservative, spoke out fearlessly on the No side. From his retirement in Perth old Walter Murdoch said, "The government is asking for . . . the power to punish a man for his beliefs—or for what some spy alleges him to believe. It will be a sad day for Australia if she allows this spiritual poison to get into her system." On the same day the prime minister assured voters that, "Nobody other than a communist can, under any conceivable circumstances, be affected." [2] Almost everyone, whatever his hopes or fears, expected an overwhelming affirmative vote, but in the event the government's proposals were narrowly defeated. Needless to say the vast majority of Australians were almost as strongly opposed to Communism as were Americans at the same period; but they were apparently less ready to sacrifice traditional liberties in the name of opposing it.

Nevertheless the Liberal–Country Party coalition was re-elected, and Menzies remained its unchallenged leader. No Australian prime minister ever ruled the country for anything like so long, or so continuous, a period. The reliable old anti-Communist drum proved of considerable help in most of the succeeding election campaigns, but at the same time the government had profited by its earlier unhappy experience with the "anti-Communist bill." It vigorously denounced Communism but skillfully avoided any further head-on confrontations with the trade-union movement, such as had brought down the Bruce-Page government. The Liberals were also helped enormously by yet another Labor "split." From 1954 onward many right-wing people deserted, or were expelled from, the Labor Party to form a strongly anti-Communist but separate group which came to be known in many states as the Democratic Labor Party. The great majority of its members and supporters were zealous Catholics, although most of their co-religionists remained faithful to the official Australian Labor Party. The D. L. P. has had very little success in having its candidates elected to federal or state parliaments, but it has been extremely effective in draining away from the A. L. P. enough votes to keep the Liberals in power.

Even without this aid, however, the Liberals would probably have continued in office for most of the post-war period. Menzies was unquestionably the ablest politician in the country, and he combined

[2] Brian Fitzpatrick, *The Australian Commonwealth* (Melbourne, 1956), p. 254.

with tenacity the ability to keep on learning from his mistakes. Under his leadership the Liberals have not been too proud to adopt, and successfully implement, some planks of their opponent's platform— full employment for instance. During the Chifley regime most Liberals felt, and some voiced, fears that really full employment for all who wanted work would have a disastrous effect on the economy. Without the competitive goad of fear, they believed, employees would work badly and national productivity would fall. Their theory was that a "small" or "moderate," but permanent, pool of unemployed—say 3 or 4 per cent of the work force—was an unpleasant but necessary part of the free enterprise system for which the Liberals stood. In 1952, not very long after the Menzies government had returned to power, there was a brief recession during which unemployment rose to about 2 per cent. Public reaction was so strong that the government, to get everyone back to work, quickly imposed drastic import restrictions and other controls which would probably have been denounced as socialist measures if imposed by their opponents. After that, succeeding Menzies governments placed almost as much emphasis as Labor did on maintaining full employment. Nor was this mere lip service to catch votes. Almost full employment continued to be a fact, except for another brief recession nearly ten years later. On that occasion a general election reduced the Liberal–Country Parties' usually comfortable majority in the lower house of 120 members to a majority of one. So sound government continued, without very much of the experimentation that might have been expected from Labor; but while expansion and full employment continued seemingly indefinitely, why change horses? Most Australians had good reason to be content.

Continued Post-War Expansion

It was sometimes hard for Australians themselves to realize the extent of the development that took place in the quarter century from 1940 to 1965. The war was the trigger rather than the cause of this enormous expansion, which continued under both Labor and anti-Labor governments. No earlier generation had "had it so good"— or so continuously. Australia continued to be the world's main supplier of wool, and in the early Fifties overseas prices rose to the staggering figure of more than £1 per lb; but the postwar period was remarkable precisely for the great diversification of the economy. To wool, wheat, meat, dairy products, and orchard produce were added many other crops. Some rice had been grown before the war, but afterward there was a considerable surplus for export. Tobacco and cotton continued to be imported, but for the first time it began to seem possible that this need not always be so. Even coffee and cocoa from New Guinea began to appear on the home market in significant quantities. For long before the war most important metals had been mined in quantities great enough to provide large export surpluses. After the war rich sources of bauxite for aluminum, and of uranium, were added to the iron, lead, tin, copper, zinc, silver, gold, and other metals already produced. The war also made Australians acutely aware of the one vital raw material which they lacked—oil. During the Fifties generous government subsidies stepped up the rate of search and at last in 1961 rich deposits were discovered in Queensland. This Mooni field was quickly developed while the search for others continued.

The discovery or development of new primary resources was overshadowed by the much greater advance in secondary industries. Between 1940 and 1960 the number of factories more than doubled, the real value of manufactured goods was multiplied by more than three, and the quantity of power applied to secondary industries increased nearly four times. Before the war durable consumer goods like cars, vacuum cleaners, washing machines, and refrigerators were mostly imported luxuries which only the well-to-do could afford. After it they became standard equipment for almost every household, and the vast majority of these and other manufactured articles were made in Australia. A healthy export trade in secondary products to New Zealand and other countries grew steadily. By 1965, except for Japan, Australia probably had the strongest and best-balanced economy of any country in the world outside Europe and North America.

In less tangible but no less important ways progress was just as striking. The great influx of European migrants probably helped to create a higher valuation of culture, in the narrower sense of the word, than was common in the Australian past. Life became much more urbanized, more complex, and more sophisticated. Between 1945 and 1965, for instance, the number of universities more than doubled and the number of undergraduate enrollments more than quadrupled. In painting, literature, and other arts some Australian work reached a mature standard which challenged comparison with work done anywhere in the world—and without any special pleading for regional values. Moreover, private citizens and public institutions began to patronize art to a degree scarcely conceivable before 1939. Instead of leaving for foreign parts where their work was appreciated, some leading intellectuals, artists, and writers even returned to live in the new Australia that appreciated them. Despite competition from mass-produced overseas books, the local publishing industry expanded sufficiently to meet most of the new demands made upon it. Most citizens were happy enough in the knowledge that progress in all these fields did not involve any falling-away from what they regarded as Australia's natural pre-eminence in tennis, swimming, and other sports. Similarly the New Australians introduced many new skills, fashions, and foods without really challenging the ancient and excellent predominance of steak-and-eggs.

Effects of the Post-War Boom

Nevertheless, there was a good deal of speculation about the extent to which the continuing wave of European migration was likely, in the long run, to change what Australians regarded as their basic national attitudes and goals. It is perhaps an indication of increasing maturity that not all of the speculation was apprehensive in character. For example, many prosperous citizens had long agreed with the multitude of visitors who declared that the average Australian was far too leisure- and pleasure-loving for either his own or the national good. Perhaps, thought these moralists, New Australians would work harder and for longer hours, so setting a good example to the government servants, the footballers, the surfers, the trade unionists, the life-savers, the coal miners, the students of sporting form, and the beer-drinkers—in fact, to the regrettably easy-going bulk of the population? Certainly a disproportionately large number of New Australians, by skill, perseverance and sheer hard work, built up large or small businesses of their own; and this helped to raise somewhat the general standard of business efficiency. More often than before it happened that a pair of shoes would be mended in a day or two rather than a week or two, or even that a building would be finished within a few weeks—rather than months or years—of the date stipulated in the contract; but by North American standards at least Australian business methods still seemed inefficient or downright slack. On the other hand, most New Australians fairly readily absorbed, in trade unions and elsewhere, the old Australian conviction that a man should work to live, but should not live to work. Teachers agreed that the New Australian children were generally completely assimilated into the general community even when, as often happened, their parents were not. Those who feared or hoped for dramatic changes as a longer term result of the massive immigration were probably wrong. American and Canadian experience of what were, proportionately, equally massive foreign migrations, suggest that sooner or later immigrants almost inevitably conform to the established ways of their new country—if not in the first generation, then in the second or third. And the sudden influx of new men, money, and ideas into Australia was not relatively as great, after all, as was that during the gold-rush decade in the middle of the last century. Then most contemporaries thought that the whole nature of Australian life was bound to be transformed, but in fact it was not.

A good many older Australians were vaguely troubled by some of the other possible effects of the long-continued post-war boom—its effects not so much on themselves, of course, as on young people. After 1940, they pointed out, a whole generation grew up without experiencing at first hand depression, war, or other hardships of former days which, in retrospect, seemed to have been so salutary. Boys and girls took it for granted that jobs would be available just as they assumed the sun would continue to rise in the east. If they wanted to go to the university, and had the ability to do so, a wide range of government scholarships was ready to make it easier for them. Among lefterly senior citizens these head-shakings were inspired partly by the feeling that there would be nothing like another good depression to make many younger voters change their political allegiance. To this extent the forebodings suggested a certain fossilizing of attitudes among Labor supporters, but it is also true that the policies of the two major parties tended to approach each other during the Fifties. More often the gloomy apprehensions merely reflected the well-founded conviction, not unusual among older people everywhere, that life was not what it had been when they were young. In fact the mental horizons of young people were not nearly as circumscribed as their fathers' had been, and this augured well for the future. For years trade with America, Japan, and other foreign countries had been increasing while the traditionally accepted trade with Britain had declined. People were growing more aware of the no longer so remote outside world beyond Australia's—and Britain's—shores. Young people were, or liked to feel they were, more sophisticated and cosmopolitan in outlook than their elders. Some of them seemed even to question the hallowed sentiments associated with the celebration of Anzac Day, while many vigorously queried the wisdom of the white Australia policy. Yet this same generation was equally often criticized by its elders for "playing it safe" and for conformism.

New Horizons

In truth it was the older generation which was being left behind by events. Nothing in recent history is so striking, and so important for humanity's future, as the rapid change taking place all over the world in race relations. In a back-handed way, perhaps, we may thank Hitler for it. In earlier wars men fought and died in the belief that their race or nation was innately superior to all other "lesser breeds without the law." During the Second World War, by their systematic and cold-blooded murder of some seven million men, women, and children for the crime of not having been born into the "master race," the Nazis demonstrated to everyone the logical end of racist delusions. Allied propaganda was not slow to point the moral. In Australia as elsewhere, through every medium of mass communication, people were taught the truth about race. The Nazis had to be defeated, *not* because they belonged to a different and supposedly inferior race or nation, but because they preached and practiced the scientifically false and ethically monstrous doctrine of "racial superiority." The effectiveness of the lesson is suggested by the speed with which almost all the groups of African and Asian peoples, formerly ruled by European powers, won or were given national independence in the twenty years following the war. It is shown too by the United States' rapid movement toward real social and economic integration of its Negro citizens, and by the similar movement in Australia toward assimilation of its aboriginal noncitizens. Yet Australia, with its New Guinea dependency, still appears before the world as one of the few surviving, old-style colonial powers, and she shares with South Africa the doubtful distinction of believing, or appearing to believe, in the principle of racial inequality. For however decent Australians may be about it, this is inevitably what the white Australia policy means in the eyes of most other nations.

Fortunately the true picture is not at all as black as it seems to most outside observers. During the war scores of thousands of Australian soldiers learned to value Asian friends in Malaya and the Indonesian archipelago. In 1951 the Menzies government took a leading part in launching the Colombo Plan under which many thousands of Asian and African students have been assisted to study at Australian universities. They have been completely accepted as equals and friends by Australian students—in a way that surprises many of the latter's parents and horrifies some surviving grandparents. Indeed, however conformist they may seem in some other respects, if we may judge by their actions Australian undergraduates feel more strongly about racial equality than about any other political issue. Incidents such as those at Sharpeville in South Africa, or Birmingham in Alabama, usually evoke student demonstrations and resolutions in Australian cities and, since they creditably feel that charity should begin at home, undergraduates frequently embarrass senior statesmen of all political parties with persistent questions about their attitudes to the white Australia policy.

Of course there is a large element of ingenuousness in the younger generation's attitude. Not all of them realize how easy it is to love all men as brothers in a country which, partly because of the long-standing exclusion policy that they deride, has no appreciable "race" or other minority problems. For whatever they are worth, recent samplings of public opinion indicate a decisive change in attitudes. Those interviewed were told that people of certain nationalities (no Australian could have any doubt about what was meant) were prohibited from settling permanently in Australia. They were then asked if they were in favor of admitting at least fifty migrants a year from each of these countries. Between 1954 and 1959 the answers changed as follows:[3]

YEAR	KEEP OUT	LET IN	NO OPINION
1954	61%	31%	8%
1956	51	42	7
1957	55	36	9
1958	45	44	11
1959	34	55	11

It should be emphasized that few or no Australians support a policy of completely unrestricted and unplanned immigration. If, say, 2,000,000 or so of India's 500 million-odd people were to immigrate over a few years, the effect on Australian living standards and folkways would obviously be catastrophically disruptive, while the effect on India's distressingly low living standards would be negligible. It is the principle and practice of absolute exclusion on "racial" grounds which is inevitably offensive to Asians and Africans, and discreditable to Australians. Those who want to abolish the policy aim at substituting a planned quota system such as those of the United States, Canada, and many other countries. There is good reason to expect that they will one day succeed. As Britain enters into closer trading partnership with European countries, the importance of trade and friendship with Asian neighbors must increasingly occupy the attention of Australian governments. Even if Britain's recent trading tendencies were to be reversed, the Commonwealth knows that its future must be increasingly conditioned by relations with Asian nations. More and more Australians are coming to believe that abandonment of the white Australia policy, at least in its historically rigid form, may be a necessary condition of that future.

The vast majority of citizens have already accepted the other, and more immediately vital, great change in external relations—those with the United States; but this does not mean that there will be no tensions between the two countries in the future. In the last century, when Great Britain was the most powerful country in the world, Aus-

[3] Immigration Reform Group, *Control or Colour Bar* (Melbourne, 1960), p. 34.

tralians generally took for granted their ultimate political and cultural dependence on her. Yet even though she was also their "mother country," they did not always love their dependent role. Indeed, as we have seen, Australian nationality sprang in large part from resentment at what many felt, with little reason, to be British domination. Now the United States has largely taken over Britain's role in the world. Ever since 1942 Australian security, in the ultimate analysis, has appeared to depend just as much on the United States as it formerly did on Britain. During 1963, for the first time, United States investments in Australian business and industry exceeded British investments. The influence of American films, phonograph records, magazines, books, and TV programs increases steadily, while that of British books and so on tends slowly to decline. Australians generally have been virtuous enough to make a modest degree of happiness out of necessity. They will never forget America's decisive role in the war with Japan. On the whole they like and admire Americans and, as official spokesmen seldom weary of repeating, the two countries have much more in common than Australia has with any other land outside the British-descended members of the British Commonwealth of Nations. Except for Canada, Australia is probably the most loyal ally America has. Yet it would be very surprising if Australians did not also feel irked by their dependent role just as, like the Americans themselves, they previously did *vis-à-vis* the land of their forefathers. In Australia as elsewhere only a rather small minority of people think very much about international relations. Those who do sometimes feel as exasperated over American exercises in "brinkmanship" and the doctrine of massive nuclear retaliation, as they feel grateful for American protection. Similarly, many Australians resent the trend toward American domination of important sectors of the national economy, even while they recognize the need for more American capital investment to help in the development of their country. Americans, after all, took just as ambivalent an attitude toward British financial influence on the United States in the last century.

There has also been something of a reversal of roles between right and left, *vis-à-vis* America. In the last century Australian liberals and nationalists were generally pro-American. The United States presented to them an image of progressive and nationalist radical democracy; but for this very reason Australian conservatives tended to damn Uncle Sam as a shoddy, revolutionary, anti-British vulgarian. Now that the United States, with its vast power and worldwide responsibilities, has become more interested in preserving the *status quo*, the Australian left is discovering an increasing affinity with welfare-state Britain, while the right tends to love the new America much more, though not to love the old country very much less. Australian history gives good ground for hoping that the complex new relationship with America will prove fruitful rather than destructive, as the complex old relationship with Britain did in the past.

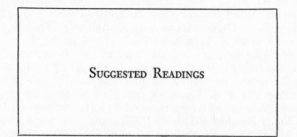

SUGGESTED READINGS

In recent years there has been some controversy among Australian historians over the so-called "Whig interpretation" of Australian history. Those who use the term believe, broadly speaking, that most Australian history has a bias to the left. It is undoubtedly true that, compared with their colleagues in the United States and Canada, or even in Britain, historians and writers in Australia do tend to be more radical or liberal in outlook; but whether this state of affairs springs naturally from the nature of Australian history as outlined in this book, or from the innate "wrong-headedness" of the writers themselves, is a question each reader must ponder for himself. It should be remembered too that such a short list as the following must be highly selective.

GENERAL HISTORIES. In 1965 the best existing short general history of Australia was probably still Sir W. Keith Hancock's *Australia* (London, 1930). This stimulating interpretative essay, incidentally, is the classic document of the "Whig" historians of Australia. Other good short histories are R. M. Crawford's *Australia* (London, 1952), Douglas Pike's *Australia: the Quiet Continent* (London, 1962) and Manning Clark's *Short History of Australia* (New York, 1963). Pike's book gives relatively more weight to the history of the smaller states, especially his native South Australia, while Clark's is both penetrating and provocative. The two best longer general histories are A. G. L. Shaw's *Story of Australia* (London, 1955) and Gordon Greenwood's *Australia: a Political and Social History* (Sydney, 1955). The latter is the more substantial but suffers, inevitably, from being the work of several hands; Greenwood, the editor, wrote three of the eight chapters. Marjorie Barnard's massive *History of Australia* (Sydney, 1962) is warm-hearted but unreliable in detail. The Australian section of the *Cambridge History of the British Empire*, Vol. 7, Part 1 (Cambridge, 1933) is still worth consulting.

Though often regarded as a general history, Russel Ward's *Australian Legend* (Melbourne, 1958) aims rather at tracing the development of the national self-image or *mystique*. In doing so it considers the application to Australia of Frederick Jackson Turner's "frontier thesis," a subject explored also in H. C. Allen's *Bush and Backwoods* (Michigan State University, 1959) and looked at briefly in Frederick Alexander's *Moving Frontiers* (Melbourne, 1947).

Manning (C. M. H.) Clark has published three invaluable collections
of documents: *Select Documents in Australian History 1788-1850* (Sydney, 1950); *Select Documents in Australian History 1851-1900* (Sydney,
1955); and *Sources of Australian History* (London, 1957).

Though all histories of Australia tend to concentrate mainly on the
history of New South Wales, especially in the period up to 1850, there
is no really satisfactory history of that state nor of any other except
Western Australia. F. K. Crowley's *Australia's Western Third* (London,
1960) provides a model which future state historians may well emulate.
Douglas Pike's *Paradise of Dissent* (Melbourne, 1957) is a scholarly and
detailed history of South Australia up until 1857, while Geoffrey Serle's
admirable *Golden Age* (Melbourne, 1963) covers the nodal decade 1851-
1861 in Victorian history. Other first-class general histories of periods in
a colony or in the country as a whole are Eris O'Brien's *Foundation of
Australia 1786-1800* (London, 1937), and the first of four volumes of
Manning Clark's projected large-scale *History of Australia,* entitled, *The
Age of Macquarie* (Melbourne, 1962). This latter covers the period from
the earliest times to 1821 and is both scholarly and imaginative in the
best sense. It has been compared with the work of Gibbon by some and
savagely attacked by others.

ECONOMIC HISTORIES. These are sometimes written in a more lively
manner than is often the case with books on "the dismal science." In his
Colonisation of Australia 1829-1842 (London, 1915), R. C. Mills gave a
sympathetic account of E. G. Wakefield's "systematic colonisation"
schemes. This work is supplemented in some respects by R. B.
Madgwick's *Immigration into Eastern Australia 1788-1851* (London,
1937). E. O. G. Shann's *Economic History of Australia* (Cambridge,
1930) is an admirably clear and stimulating work written from a conservative viewpoint, while Brian Fitzpatrick's *British Imperialism and
Australia 1783-1833* (London, 1939) and *The British Empire in Australia 1834-1939* (Melbourne, 1941) cover the same ground in greater
detail and from a radical socialist angle. Fitzpatrick's *Australian People*
(Melbourne, 1946) is a shorter work, social rather than economic in its
emphasis, while his *Australian Commonwealth 1901-1955* (Melbourne,
1956) is a lively if loosely organized book, invaluable to those interested
in civil liberties. J. A. LaNauze's *Political Economy in Australia* (Melbourne, 1949) is a brief but important study of three economists including "King David" Syme, the apostle of protection in Victoria in the
second half of the nineteenth century. S. J. Butlin's *Foundations of the
Australian Monetary System 1788-1851* (Melbourne, 1953) and his
brother N. G. Butlin's *Investment in Australian Economic Growth
1861-1900* (London, 1963) are the most considerable later works in the
field. Both pay tribute to Fitzpatrick's pioneering work, while dissenting
from his conclusions.

In recent years there have appeared many good books covering the
history of an industry or even of a single important business institution.
Among the most important are Alan Barnard's *Australian Wool Market*

1840-1900 (Melbourne, 1958) and his *Visions and Profits: Studies in the Business Career of Thomas Sutcliffe Mort* (Melbourne, 1961), Edgars Dunsdorfs' *Australian Wheat-Growing Industry* (Melbourne, 1956), S. J. Butlin's *Australian and New Zealand Bank* (Melbourne, 1961), and L. F. Giblin's *Growth of a Central Bank* (Melbourne, 1951). Geoffrey Blainey's books in this field are entertaining as well as scholarly. *Gold and Paper* (Melbourne, 1959) is a history of the National Bank of Australasia. *Peaks of Lyell* (Melbourne, 1954) traces the development of gold and base-metal mining in western Tasmania, while *The Rush That Never Ended* (Melbourne, 1963) shows the importance of the mining industry for Australian development after the mid-century Victorian gold rush was over. Blainey also published the admirable *Centenary History of the University of Melbourne* (Melbourne, 1957).

BIOGRAPHIES. In this field H. M. Ellis is the outstanding writer. His three major books are *Lachlan Macquarie* (Sydney, 1947), *Francis Greenway* (Sydney, 1949), and *John Macarthur* (Sydney, 1955), and it is understood that Ellis' life of *William Charles Wentworth* is almost ready for publication. H. V. Evatt's important *Rum Rebellion* (Sydney, 1938), though not a biography, is mentioned here for its treatment of the characters of Macquarie, Macarthur, and William Bligh. Evatt's view of these men conflicts with that of Ellis. Evatt's *Australian Labour Leader* (Sydney, 1940) is a sympathetic but scholarly biography of W. A. Holman, the New South Wales Labor leader before and during the 1914-1918 war. Other important biographies include George Mackaness's *Life of Vice-Admiral Sir William Bligh* (London, 1931) and his *Life of Admiral Arthur Phillip* (London, 1937), Margaret Kiddle's *Caroline Chisholm* (Melbourne, 1950), Kathleen Fitzpatrick's *Sir John Franklin in Tasmania* (Melbourne, 1949), J. V. Barry's *Alexander Maconochie of Norfolk Island* (Melbourne, 1958), and L. F. Crisp's warmly sympathetic study of *Ben Chifley* (Melbourne, 1961). W. Farmer Whyte's *William Morris Hughes: His Life and Times* (Sydney, 1957) is a cheerful but uncritical work.

Under the leadership of Sir W. Keith Hancock and Douglas Pike at the Australian National University, hundreds of contributors are currently preparing a multi-volume *Australian Dictionary of Biography.* Meanwhile the best existing works of this sort are P. Serle's *Dictionary of Australian Biography* (2 vols., Sydney, 1949) and the *Australian Encyclopedia* (10 vols., Sydney, 1958).

POLITICAL HISTORY. Any list of books on Australian political, legal, or constitutional history must reflect the so-called "Whig" emphasis. Among the most interesting may be mentioned Myra Willard's *History of the White Australia Policy* (Melbourne, 1923), A. T. Yarwood's *Asian Migration to Australia: the Background to Exclusion 1896-1923* (Melbourne, 1964), J. T. Sutcliffe's *History of Trade Unionism in Australia* (Melbourne, 1921), the great pre-historian V. Gordon Childe's *How Labour Governs* (London, 1923), H. V. Evatt's *The King and His Dominion Governors* (London, 1936), L. F. Crisp's *Parliamentary Govern-*

ment of the Commonwealth of Australia (London, 1949) and his *Australian Federal Labour Party* (London, 1955), Geoffrey Sawer's twin volumes *Australian Federal Politics and Law 1901-1929* and *1929-1950* (Melbourne, 1956 and 1962), Frederick Eggleston's *Reflections of an Australian Liberal* (Melbourne, 1953), J. M. Ward's *Earl Grey and the Australian Colonies 1846-1857* (Melbourne, 1958), and Gordon Greenwood's *Future of Australian Federalism* (Melbourne, 1946). R. A. Gollan's *Radical and Working Class Politics: a Study of Eastern Australia 1850-1910* (Melbourne, 1960) is quite as much social as political in treatment.

EXTERNAL RELATIONS. Among the relatively few books published in this field four may be mentioned: Gordon Greenwood's *Early Australian-American Relations* (Melbourne, 1944), J. D. Legge's *Australian Colonial Policy* (Sydney, 1956), C. D. Rowley's *Australians in New Guinea 1914-1921* (Melbourne, 1958), and the American scholar C. Hartley Grattan's *The United States and the Southwest Pacific* (Cambridge, Mass., Oxford, and Melbourne, 1961).

THE LAND. The history of land settlement has been not less important in Australia than in other "new countries" like the United States. The two major works in this field are S. H. Roberts' *History of Australian Land Settlement* (Melbourne, 1924) and his *Squatting Age in Australian History* (Melbourne, 1935). Though not very satisfactory in some ways, neither book has yet been replaced by a better. Three valuable accounts of pioneer squatting life in different districts and periods are Marnie Bassett's *The Hentys* (Melbourne, 1954), Margaret Kiddle's *Men of Yesterday* (Melbourne, 1961), and Mary Durack's *Kings in Grass Castles* (London, 1962). Kathleen Fitzpatrick's *Australian Explorers* (Melbourne, 1958) gives a good short guide to the history of land exploration and some well-chosen extracts from the diaries of leading explorers.

EDUCATION AND THE ARTS. Two excellent books on the history of education are now available, A. G. Austin's *Australian Education 1788-1900* (Melbourne, 1961) and Ronald Fogarty's *Catholic Education in Australia 1806-1950* (2 vols., Melbourne, 1959). The first is written from a secular viewpoint and the second from a Roman Catholic one, but both are thoroughly scholarly and temperate works.

The most important guides to Australian writing are H. M. Green's *History of Australian Literature 1789-1950* (2 vols., Sydney, 1961) and Cecil Hadgraft's shorter *Australian Literature* (London, 1960). In his *Australian Tradition* (Melbourne, 1958) A. A. Phillips expounds the nationalist tradition in writing, while Vincent Buckley's *Essays in Poetry; Mainly Australian* (Melbourne, 1957) is a good example of the opposed "universalist" criticism. Three handy anthologies are the *Penguin Books —of Australian Verse, Australian Ballads,* and *Australian Folksongs.*

The best history of Australian art is Bernard Smith's *Australian Painting 1788-1960* (Melbourne, 1963). Those wishing to dig deeper should consult also the same author's scholarly and penetrating *European Vision and the South Pacific 1768-1850* (Oxford, 1960).

JOURNALS AND GUIDES. Two journals, each issued twice a year, print between them much if not most of the published research work in Australian history. They are *Historical Studies: Australia and New Zealand* published from the University of Melbourne, and the *Australian Journal of Politics and History* published from the University of Queensland. Two good longer surveys—or guides—to the broad field of Australian historiography may also be mentioned: K. A. MacKirdy's "Clio's Australian Accent: Main Trends of Recent Historical Writing in Australia," in *The Canadian Historical Association Report*, 1958, pp. 77-98; and J. M. Ward's chapter on "Historiography" in *The Pattern of Australian Culture*, ed. A. L. McLeod (Ithaca and Melbourne, 1963), pp. 195-251. *Meanjin Quarterly*, published from the University of Melbourne, keeps its readers abreast of developments in all the arts.

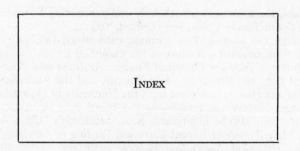

INDEX